THE E(

STOCK MARKEI

ENJOY !

DAVID -

THE ECSTATIC STOCK MARKET

A DISCERNING LOOK AMID AN AMAZING TIME.

DAVID RASMUSSEN

ISBN 978-1-7372515-2-1

Table of Contents

Epigraph

Nothingness can be said to be Zero.
Zero births One.
One created Two.
Two births Three.
After that, only Zero can count what it Is.
But all breathe the Air of Nothingness...
Begin counting again, but commence from Infinity.

Tao Te Ching– Verse 42
translation by Jeremy M. Miller, 2013)

Introduction

The Challenge

History doesn't repeat but it rhymes. -- attributed to Mark Twain.

October 19, 1987. So-called "Black Monday." The U.S. stock market fell 22.3% in one day. Creating the largest daily percentage drop ever.

In prior history, atomic bombs exploded on Japan. Two world wars raged. The great depression crippled the nation. Periods of high inflation and deflation came and went. We endured famines, smallpox outbreaks, dust bowls, massive earthquakes, and deadly hurricanes. A major civil war ravaged the nation. We witnessed murdered presidents and world leaders. Bank runs, savings and loan crises, energy crises, and deadly terrorist attacks all impacted the stock market.

What transpired on this day? What left the market worth $1 trillion less than 24 hours before?

A quick scan of the news. Something worse than the previous must be crossing the wires. Perhaps nuclear war with Russia? A minor asteroid hit? Yellowstone volcano erupting? The magnetic poles shifted? A major solar flare knocked out the power grid? A UFO invasion? Well, let's see, hmm… nothing! The only news of relevance, the market itself.

This turn of events was baffling, fascinating, and motivating. I resolved to discover what was happening here!

Fast forward over 3 decades of an incredible ride and here is my report on what the stock market has to convey.

The book contains four parts.

Part One lays out a prediction for the equity market for the next 30 years.

Part Two contains other thinkers who arrived at similar conclusions - or frameworks.

Part Three comprises my interpretation of the message beyond stock prices.

Part Four closes with some practical applications.

The market is communicating a missive beyond dollars and cents. It is encapsulating how evolution is unfolding and our place in it. I started by seeking to understand the crash of 1987 and determine if it was predictable. Not only was it predictable, the market provided the prediction.

Part One

The Journey.

The cave you fear to enter holds the treasure that you seek. - Joesph Campbell.

M arket predictions are an ambitious game. John Templeton — an icon in the money management field for over 55 years — said this regarding stock market predictions. "The influence on stock prices are so numerous and so complex that no person has ever been able to predict the trend of stock prices with consistent success."

So, making a 30-year prediction about the stock market sounds ridiculous. Yet, that's what I present here.

I contend this complexity contains an underlying simplicity, thus enabling success at producing forecasts. For the first time in history, we have enough data, computer power, and understanding of complex systems to unlock this simplicity.

In part One, I go on record with this 30-year forecast, and assert the reason it's relevant, valid, and timely, and present the genesis.

Chapter 1

Down the Rabbit Hole.

Why waste my time listening to half-truths, shadowy statements, inaccurate projections, and just plain bold-faced lies? I could just look at the behavior of the stock. The story was clear in its action. The truth was in the tape for anyone and everyone to see. - Jesse Livermore.

The fabric of stock market culture weaves with venerable old sayings. Like, "the fastest way to have a million dollars in your investment account is to start with two million."

Invest or trade and prepare for humility. We learn the genesis for so many sayings and books around the markets.

If we think we're intelligent, attempt to match wits with the markets. If we think we understand who we are, have a dance with the psychology of the financial markets. One of the first messages we hear, is the markets are larger than us. They are also bigger than everyone.

The Federal Reserve might think they can control the markets, they can't. Presidents might think their power holds dominion over the market, it doesn't. We might surmise our elected officials are on top of things and in charge, they are not.

Anyone can come into the marketplace and influence its behavior for a brief period. Yet, "go where the markets want to go, not where you want them to go." Sayings like this are popular around Wall Street for a reason. It's what the participants discover.

It turns out chaos theory, and the modern science of complexity, assist in the explanation. Sometimes referred to as the field of CAS. This acronym stands for the study of Complex Adaptive Systems. Stay with me. This is not a textbook. But we need to cover some basics, enabling a language to proceed with.

What is a Complex Adaptive System? It is any interconnecting system with inputs adapting to those inputs. This includes power grids, our brain, social networks, ant colonies, cities, traffic flows, cells, and the stock market.

Books on chaos theory, complexity theory, and the markets, already exist. My aim points elsewhere. First, I want to create something practical and relatable. I want to leave the science on the surface and keep the math simple. I'm not seeking to get deep into how or why it works. It seems more valuable and enjoyable to present the findings, and help you, the reader, profit from what I have learned.

Complexity sounds like a big word doesn't it? Yet at it's core, it holds an ironic message of simplicity. It agrees with Thoreau's musing from "Walden:" *'Our life is frittered away by detail. Simplify, simplify, simplify! I say, let your affairs be as two or three, and not a hundred or a thousand.'*

We don't need to appreciate why the meteorologist is predicting a Category 5 hurricane is about to make landfall. We need to understand its implications for us and our direct course of action. Is it best if we:

A) stay put with supplies on hand,
B) evacuate until the storm passes, or
C) evacuate and prepare to move because destruction awaits our home.

So let's accept the stock market is a complex system, and distill it down to a few simple concepts we can all relate with. We merely need to understand a few basic points; attractors, bifurcation points and fractals.

Complex systems, like the stock market, have attractors. These attractors pull the market in a direction. They also have bifurcation points. These act as a shift towards a new attractor. And they perform these characteristics in a fractal or self-similar fashion.

Envision a coin drop spiral wishing well you see at a carnival or the mall. After you release a coin into the bowl, it swirls around and finds its way to the bottom. The basin is the attractor. Now imagine once it falls out of the hole in the bottom, rather than turning into a gumball, the coin falls into one of many other wishing wells moving about below it.

The fall from one bowl to the next is a bifurcation; a change in direction towards a different attractor.

Now imagine, every wishing well also acts as a coin inside of a larger well. Therefore, coins of various sizes are rolling around and falling into other larger wells. These larger wells do the same thing. The small wishing well mirrors a coin spinning inside a much bigger wishing well. And so on, and so on. Wishing wells, inside of wishing wells, inside of even bigger wishing wells.

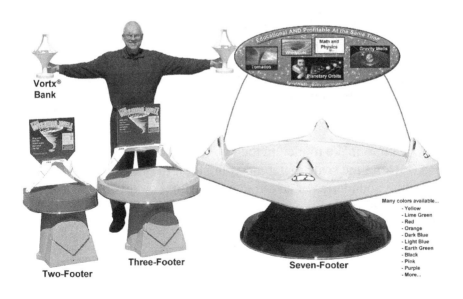

All the wells spin towards their attractors as they bifurcate into different trajectories.

In the stock market, this transpires as players from all time frames, pocketbooks, and agendas, participate in an arena containing enormous rewards and considerable power. These players include market-makers, gamblers, speculators, day-traders, investors, entrepreneurs, corporate raiders, and crooks. Add to this, groups like pension funds, banks, dark pools, hedge funds, mutual funds, and governments. All operating in diverse time frames and optimizing their own best interests. Think of these as the various size bowls or wishing wells.

The specialist on the floor of the New York Stock Exchange sets the bid/offer price throughout the day. This works as a small bowl, moving the price, as orders come into the market.

The Federal Reserve fixes the cost of money by adjusting the amount of its supply in the banking system. This works like a large bowl.

Each bowl acts like the vortex of a wishing well. Pulling the market into its basin of attraction.

Once understood, these attractors kill any ideas we have about blaming the market or its participants for our results. No conspiracy controls the stock market. No Wizard of Oz hides behind the curtain. There may, or may not, be cabals acting as serious players, but they all live inside a bowl while moving some smaller bowls into their vortex of control. But, if they fight their higher vortex, they will lose.

If you want to make money in the market, I have some encouraging news. Pick a time scale matching your strengths and personality. Locate the boundaries of an attractor operating on this time scale. Set up some solid risk parameters for the scale, then get on board and you will win. Like the wishing well. Create a reliable algorithm repeating this, and you too will become a titan. Simple enough.

Be careful not to confuse simple with easy. Rather, it is constructive to simplify the process.

You might think, "I don't work on Wall Street nor do I know how to write algorithms. How can any of this CAS talk benefit me?" Let's begin here:

Chapter 2

Patterns Within Patterns

There's more to the picture than meets the eye, hey hey, my my. Neil Young.

C omplexity dictates the stock market holds self-similarity at its core. The technical term is invariant, meaning similar rules govern at all scales. We can simplify this and say it's fractal.

When we construct a graph of market price and plot it over time, we create a chart of its price. It's impossible to tell if we're looking at a one-minute chart, a daily chart, or a yearly chart. All time scales appear the same. For an illustration of this, notice the book's cover.

The cover captures 741 years of wheat prices, 68 years of the S&P 500, and 10 years of Tesla's stock price.

The first rule, presented in Chapter 1, was: pick a time scale matching our personality. What do I mean by time scale?

Here is a quick breakdown of market time scales:

-Market maker — focus on milliseconds
-Day trader - focus on days
-Speculator - focus on weeks
-Investor - focus on quarters
-Institution - focus on years
-Governments - focus on decades

Warren Buffett has amassed a fortune exceeding 100 billion dollars. He created his wealth as a keen long-term investor. He claims his favorite holding period is forever.

Blair Hull sold his firm to Goldman Sachs in 1999 for 531 million dollars. He focused on the change in the bid-offer spread happening in milliseconds.

They both produced impressive profitability, operating in the markets from divergent points of view. They both execute well and stick to their time scale; they don't drift. By drift, I mean sliding from one scale to another.

A day trader carrying their position into a different time scale will become one of the vast majority who fails. If their trade is going against them, and they decide to keep it longer, they have drifted towards speculation. When they are wrong, they will lose more than the small profits they pick up during the day. Also, if the first time they show even a small profit they grab it, they have drifted into the territory of the market maker. This shorter scale comes with a different set of rules and transaction costs.

So, pick a time scale fitting your strengths, then master that scale and stick to it. Warren Buffett and Blair Hull have evolved, but they have understood what time scale they were on.

Mr. Buffett appears condescending on any time scale but his. His partner Charlie Munger states short-term traders are negative to the system. This, in part, explains his success as an investor. It illustrates how devoted he is to that scale; he doesn't even believe in the validity of other scales. Thus, he doesn't drift.

Time scale is paramount to trading/investing success. It's also paramount to making predictions.

As humans, we constantly predict. A high number of the predictions we create are of the linear variety. These include catching a baseball or managing a budget. However, catching a deflating balloon, or trading the stock market, need nonlinear predictions to succeed.

Complex systems are nonlinear. And for making predictions in a nonlinear system, the time scale matters. What size bowl are we predicting in; remember bowls within bowls. Also, how established has the trajectory become within the bowl?

A fantastic example of valid predictions of a complex system is the weather. One or two days out, we can predict with a remarkable level of accuracy. This short-term prediction aids in knowing what to wear on any given day. It's accurate enough to inform us if we need to bring an umbrella.

A couple of months from now, we can predict a range for the weather. We can't tell with the same accuracy what the exact conditions will be 42 days from now, but we can predict the range. This doesn't illuminate about the umbrella for any day, yet the accuracy assists us in knowing when to plant crops or to place orders for our winter clothes.

Mix these scales up, and we capture erroneous results. Same with the bowls. The closer the coin is to the release or the bottom of the bowl, the more reliable prediction we can calculate about its short-term trajectory. Predictions of the entire trajectory remain elusive.

With nonlinear systems, you can sometimes predict short-term, but not long-term. However, **short-term and long-term become relative.**

We can't predict the exact path of a hurricane until it is well-established. Once it has formed, our supercomputers produce accurate short-term forecasts and predictions.

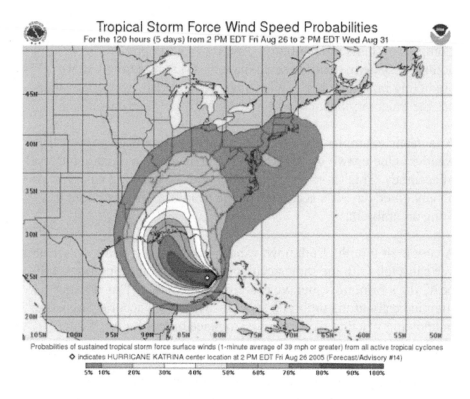

Tropical Storm Force Wind Speed Probabilities
For the 120 hours (5 days) from 2 PM EDT Fri Aug 26 to 2 PM EDT Wed Aug 31

Probabilities of sustained tropical storm force surface winds (1-minute average of 39 mph or greater) from all active tropical cyclones
◇ indicates HURRICANE KATRINA center location at 2 PM EDT Fri Aug 26 2005 (Forecast/Advisory #14)

5% 10% 20% 30% 40% 50% 60% 70% 80% 90% 100%

We also produce accurate forecasts about the hurricane season.

The prediction of hurricane season is short-term for anyone looking at it on a yearly time scale. The prediction is possible because it is also well-established within this time frame.

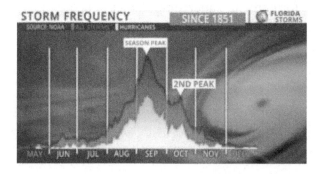

It changes the game for creating successful predictions to understand these points. So let's recap. First, the system must be complex. Second, it must be established. Third, we must understand the time scale we're operating on.

I will explain by using a classic example in chaos literature, a ball, and water.

If we drop a ball in a river and attempt to predict its exact path down the river, we will fail. Water flows in a complex or chaotic manner. The butterfly effect, or the initial set of conditions, will be in full force. Where and when we place the ball creates different outcomes every time.

If we release the ball in the current, right near a rock in the middle of the river, accurate short-term predictions become possible. The rock creates an attractor by forming a predictable amount of surface flow. The prediction will only hold during the period the rock affects the water flow.

If we release a ball, from the same position next to the rock, 100 times and map the trajectory, we will never replicate the exact path. Yet, we will map a similar path every time. The rock is an attractor, but a strange one; i.e. not perfect. Thus, the term, a 'strange attractor.'

Now let's drop 1000 balls in the river with a GPS tracking device on every ball. If we graph an average of all 1000 trajectories, it will create a map of the surface flow of the river. Some balls won't make it down the river. Others will bounce around an eddy. But if we have enough balls, where most of them arrive down the path of the river, and we average the trajectory, we have a chart.

If we repeat the 1000 balls 100 times, we get a map capturing the strange attractor of the river itself. This map would hold a prediction much longer than the rock did. On its time scale, it too will only be valid short-term. Because when the river hits the ocean or any larger flow, the average of the 1000 balls would bifurcate.

Let's perform the same thing with trillions of water molecules. Drop them from the sky over our river, then monitor clusters of molecules, then average those clusters. Then map a trajectory of those clusters. We create a map of a strange attractor on a larger scale. Thus, capturing the groundwater levels, the fractal tributaries, and the delta as it moves into the ocean. Once again, it would break apart as the system dissipates.

If we do this again with every water molecule on the surface of the planet, by creating a snapshot of all of them. Then start a process mapping the trajectory of every one of those. We get an accurate picture of the evaporation cycle, cloud formation, jet stream, and ocean currents. Once again, its properties hold short term. This surface area will also dissipate. We would need new inputs because we simply dealt with the surface water, not all the water in the system.

Notice how the rock gave us a prediction lasting in seconds. The river gave us a prediction lasting minutes. The basin and delta gave us one lasting hours. The entire surface provided one in days. Every prediction held short-term. Every prediction dissipated long term. The time horizon separated the successful layers.

All these horizons meet our criteria. All were complex systems. All were established. And we understood the time scale we were operating on.

Spoiler alert. The stock market operates in this manner.

Scales of attractors underlay the system.

At each level, short-term predictions become valid, and long-term predictions remain invalid. But as we have learned, time is relative. Therefore, I will illustrate how **30 years is short-term, and therefore valid, viewed from the proper scale.** First, let's do some leg work.

Chapter 3

Analogs vs. Fractals. And the Winner is...

Sometimes gain comes from losing, and sometimes loss comes from gaining. - Lao Tzu

Look at these 6 charts. They appear similar, don't they. Well, they should, because they all have over a 95% correlation. If you're a statistician, you understand the high relationship signaled by this number. For us non-statisticians, let's have a concise description.

Correlation measures the extent that two variables change together without making a statement about cause and effect. 100% means they are identical. 0% means they have no relationship.

One of these charts is three months from start to finish. There is a two-year, two five-year, one ten-year, and one that is 100 years long.

Chart 3-1

Chart 3-2

Chart 3-3

Chart 3-4

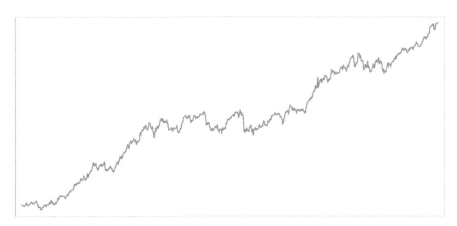

Chart 3-5

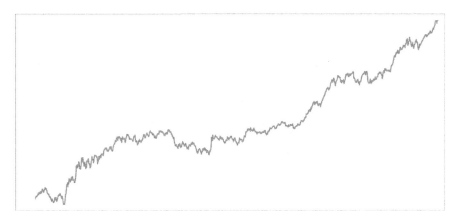

Chart 3-6

The charts were constructed with U.S. stock market indexes. Three finished in 1929, and three completed in 1987.

I took off the labels, illustrating how problematic it is to know the scale.

They are scale-invariant.

When we superimpose the five-year chart from 1929 on top of the five-year chart from 1987, the comparison stands out.

Chart 3-7

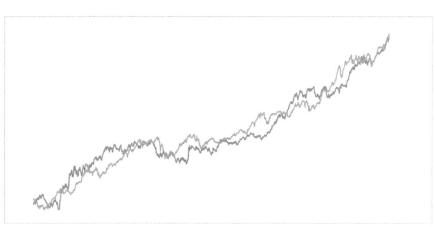

Witness the analog overlay chart with folklore status on Wall Street, made famous by Paul Tudor Jones. It was his road-map for trading the boom and crash of 1987. They attribute it to Peter Borish, who worked with Tudor Investments.

At first glance, it appears to have cleared up what transpired in 1987. It was the market repeating itself. However, consider what took place afterward.

Chart 3-8

The break came on schedule. The correlation held, and then it broke apart. For five years, this was an awesome road map. Why did it work, and why did it stop? Looks like significant effort remains to solve the 1987 problem.

So let's peer deeper. Fractals are at play, and that's why they look so similar.

Almost everything in nature contains fractals. Examples include our brains, lungs, and blood vessels. Also, snowflakes, coastlines, clouds, and mountains. (See Chapter 21 for some illustrations) Let's use trees to illustrate how 1929 and 1987 are acting like fractals.

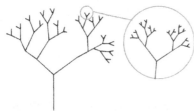

The top of the chart acts as a leaf. By looking at the leaf, we see the entire tree in a miniature pattern. So for our analogy, 1929 has three parts. Chart 4 is the leaf (5 years), chart 5 is the branch (10 years) and chart 6 is the whole tree (100 years). Then for 1987, chart 1 is the leaf (3 months), chart 2 is the branch (2 years) and chart 3 is the tree (5 years.)

The move ending in1929, explains its own structure. And the same holds for 1987 with itself.

So, what's explaining the similarity between 1929 and 1987? Well, it is scale.

Let me illustrate: I will make two changes to chart 7. Both involve scale. First, let's adjust the time scale of 1987 by speeding it up relative to 1929. Then let's log the results.

So how does this new overlay look?

Chart 3-9

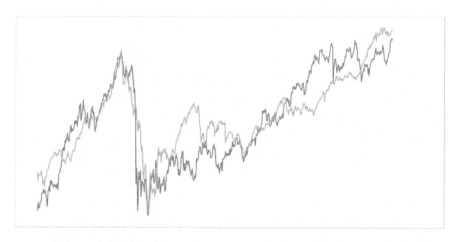

Similar strong correlation, but now we see why Tudor Jones overlay stopped working. The sped-up crash of 1987 fractals (mirrored) the **entire bear market** of 1929-1932. It appeared like the top as well, because of its fractal nature.

The leaf of 1929 was the tree of 1987.

The leaf of 1929 looks like the branches and the tree of 1929. The leaf of 1987 looks like the branches and the tree of 1987. The leaf of 1929 looked like the leaf of 1987. The pertinent comparison was the leaf of 1929 to the tree of 1987.

1987 and 1929 both were exhibiting fractal behavior to themselves and toward each other. And 1987 was moving faster than 1929.

Here lie the seeds of putting it all together.

Chapter 4

Bulls and Bears.

As above, so below. - Hermetic text

The next graph shows a chart of the SP500 stock index from 1929 to 1966, and a chart of the SP500 from 2007 to Feb 2021. Once again, I have sped up the recent chart and scaled the two. 37 and 14 years for the respective periods.

Chart 4-1

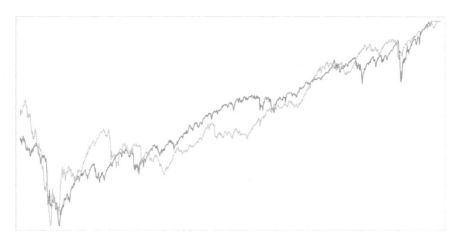

These two series are 93% correlated. The similarities extend beyond the price movement.

At the start of the first period - the gray line - we have the famous "Great Depression." In the second period - the black line - we have the famous "Great Recession."

Another example of a message of the stock market. A comparable period with similar price movements and related economic forces at play. The more recent period moves faster in time and smaller in absolute magnitude. The Great Depression lasted 4 years, had 25% unemployment and a 30% reduction in GDP. The Great Recession lasted 1 year, had 10% unemployment and a 4.7% reduction in GDP.

We see another similarity between World War II vs the War on Terror. Both changed the landscape and controlled the news. Once again, with less violence and fewer deaths. As terrible as the War on Terror felt, it was nowhere near as deadly and bleak as WWII.

Late in the chart, observe a sharp spike down in both periods. In 1962, this coincided with the Cuban Missile crisis. In 2020, it's the COVID-19 crisis. The market broke and rebounded similarly in both instances. Notice the similarities in the social mood during the period now, and the mood of the mid-1960s. Civil unrest and civil rights issues coalesce at the forefront in both periods. The progress comes easier, faster, and with less destruction.

Television and modern media hit the scene during the 1929 to 1966 period. Great media empires get built. Fortunes got amassed, while people change how we move information around as it speeds up.

Concerns accompanied these changes. In 1961, Newton Minow went before the nation and quoted Bartlow Martin and called television the "vast wasteland."

During our recent 14-year period, social media hit the scene. Once again, new empires formed and fortunes amassed. And also, people changed the method of movement for information as the speed continued to accelerate. And by 2020, a documentary film, "The Social Dilemma", sounds the alarm of this new media.

The pattern rhymes. The network builds on itself. And it's adding layers of complexity as it goes. And it's doing it faster and faster.

A remarkable mathematical relationship underlies these two periods. And keep in mind, the added layer of fractals. Thus, these two periods also coincide with other similar historical periods.

In media, for example, as we continue to spiral backward, we hit the telegraph and Morse code in the 1840s. We repeat the process, and we behold the printing press in 1440. Again, and we arrive at movable type in 1040. Apply the math again, and we get woodblock printing in the 3rd Century. It doesn't stop there. As we implement the math again, we contact the Greek Alphabet in 800 BC. Let's do it anew, and the first written literature in Sumerian shows up in 2500 BC, in a perfect mathematical relationship to all the other periods.

Drums arrive in Africa around 6000 BC, the next mathematical relationship. Possibly a type of media and information sharing technology? Cave painting and language itself have a ratio relationship with these periods as well.

We will explore this line of thinking further in Chapter 8, so let's get back to our comparison and what the late 1960s says about the near future.

Looking forward, we create some projections for the next few years. Watch for waves of sideways action in the stock indexes. During this sideways period, some individual stocks will have terrific moves. Speculative fever will be in specific stocks, not the indexes. The Yin and Yang of passive vs active will swing towards the active. The seeds are planted and growing. The rise of Reddit and social media boards has taken hold and has put the professionals on notice.

1932 to 1966 was a period of low-interest rates and deflationary forces. Then came the 1970s with rising rates and inflationary forces. The low rates and deflationary pressures of the last 14 years will give way to rising rates and inflation.

Commodities had tremendous runs in the 1970s. Watch for significant moves again in the coming few years.

Psychedelics hit the scene in the late 1960s. Watch for a wave of resurgence in the next few years. Already we see Joe Rogan, Micheal Polin, and Sam Harris pushing this mainstream. Even a psychedelic mushroom company has gone public in Canada.

We had an environmental movement in the late 1960s, and watch for the green new deal to pick up steam.

A space race in the previous period captured society. Now, Space X, Blue Origin, and Virgin Orbit are all queued up to play their part in the next one. Last time it was governments racing it out, this time global titans joined in.

Crime and urban decay were an unpleasant part of the late 60s and early 70s. It appears it's happening again.

The previous period was the "Pivot of Change," and now the "Great Reset."

I hope this frame helps your prosperity grow from embracing these trends. But I also hope it helps remove anxiety from how uncertain things appear. It has happened before as a necessary component of the march forward. It will be painful, but it will pass. And from it, we will learn what's necessary to evolve and set the stage for the next wave of advancement.

Chapter 5

The Long and Winding Road.

God it's so painful something that's so close and still so far out of reach. - "American Girl." - Tom Petty.

A n overview of how I got here might prove beneficial. In the mid-1980s, when I was first getting my feet wet with the markets, I loved reading everything I could get my hands on. This was before the internet, so it was reading books and hanging out in the library. CNBC didn't even exist. Print news and public television provided the only source for business news.

As the bull market picked up steam, a man named Robert Prechter got a following. He had been bullish; the market was going up, so people listened. I thought his ideas sounded quack-ish. I thought "fundamentals" ruled the market, and "chartist's" or "technicians" were charlatans.

I respected Paul Tudor Jones - whom I've already mentioned - intellectual views on the market.He was making big money and had an admirable, fundamental understanding of how the economy and markets worked. Then one day, to my surprise, I read Mr. Jones saying Robert Prechter was "the best".

I figured I had two choices with this information. I could lose some respect for Tudor Jones's views, or I could look closer into the "Elliott Wave Theory." So I checked into Mr. Prechter and Mr. Elliott's Theory.

Long before Benoit Mandelbrot (see Chapter 21) coined the word fractal, Ralph Elliott was finding them in the stock market. His observations pushed the ball down the court towards the markets being understood as nonlinear.

Observe his representation of the fractal nature of the market written in 1940.

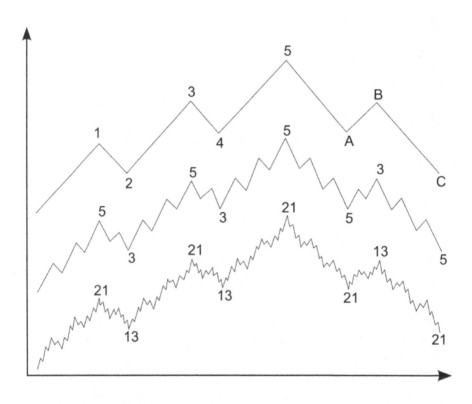

Each scale has the same pattern. He claims this one pattern governs the entire market.

As I read his works, I had a weighty issue I couldn't get past. It seemed too subjective and difficult to quantify. You study a chart, and then 'count' what wave you are in.

This frame provides an excellent way to view the structure of the market. Yet, even if correct, I didn't understand how I could make money by applying it. It seemed subjective.

So, I moved past his subjective counting of waves and used this framework as a stepping stone to go more concrete and mathematical. However, Elliott also set an immense trap for me. His work centered on the golden mean, or Fibonacci ratio, as the math of the market.

Much has been written about the Fibonacci sequence, and so I have nothing of value to add here. For anyone who is not familiar with it, I'll give a brief explanation. Each number contains the sum of the preceding two numbers. Thus,: 0,1,1,2,3,5,8,13,21,34,55,89 etc.

This pattern of growth abounds in nature. Famous examples include pine cones, sunflowers, and the nautilus shell. The ratio of two numbers over each preceding number settles in at 1.618, known as the golden ratio.

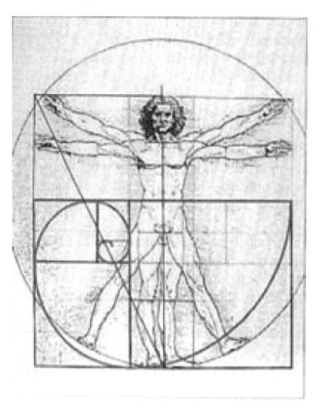

For years, I experimented with market overlays using this ratio. Sometimes the results were encouraging. Data was difficult to come by, and computers were much slower. Calculations taking only a few minutes with today's computers took overnight with the best computer I could buy.

This entire journey lasted over a decade. During this time, I was making excellent money as a market maker at the Chicago Board of Trade and the Chicago Mercantile Exchange. Between not making any progress on how to apply chaos to the markets, coupled with earning money elsewhere, I ended up putting the project on the back burner. But I never stopped trying to figure it out.

A significant breakthrough came when I hit a bump in the road on the market-making side of things.

Technology started displacing all kinds of traders at the exchanges while opening new opportunities for the flash boys. - This is a reference to Michael Lewis's book, "The Flash Boys," which chronicles the game-changing technology hitting the exchanges. - This game proved too expensive for my skill set and or pocketbook, so time to understand the missing chaos piece.

All signs pointed towards being on to something relevant. However, I had no urgency to flush out what was missing. I saw a similar thread running through various fields, but I still wasn't able to put the eye of the pyramid into place.

It's hard to describe how this felt. I could see, by speeding up and slowing down time scales, there appeared a universal order. But finding a universal input remained elusive. Common logic might dismiss it as possible. But the market was saying otherwise.

It seemed possible I might have been falling into a bias. We, humans, find patterns so well, we locate ones that don't even exist. Yet, we believe they are genuine. Apophenia can present itself when viewing stock charts.

Gambler's fallacy contains another common human bias. It states we hold greater importance to data reinforcing our view but dismisses the data which doesn't fit our view. We remember when we correctly made a wager, and recall when we were right but didn't bet. But we fail to add up all the times we were wrong or didn't bet when they were wrong.

I'll share a few more biases I knew were in the path.

There is the Dunning-Kruger effect. This is where fools are blind to their own foolishness.

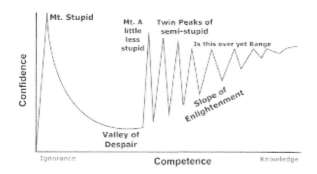

Ironically, in a bull market, this can be a plus. Old timers know too much. The rookies without the battle scars can be bold enough to ride the bull. But, when the bear comes out of the cave, they will get introduced to the 'valley of despair.'

Other traps included holy grail hunting which provides a path to your trading/investing graveyard. While, "ride winners, cut losers, manage risk," are the rules to live by. However, I could observe universality in the market. And this universality appeared worth pursuing. So I pressed on.

Data mining and curve fitting are also slippery slopes in market system building. But multifractal, scaling, and power laws helped confirm if I was over-fitting the data, so I pressed on.

The best way to avoid the traps sat in getting the math to add up. Until then, I had to concede, the naysayers had the edge. Then everything shifted once I produced an obvious change. Well, obvious in hindsight, because it involved using a universal constant in nonlinear bifurcation diagrams.

I started using the Feigenbaum constants.

In 1975, Mitchell Feigenbaum discovered - much to his amazement - all bifurcation systems share a constant period doubling ratio of approximately 4.6692. The financial markets do the same. It was a eureka. The puzzle pieces fell into place.

Time to write this book.

Chapter 6

Cooking with Crisco.

The markets are like sex. It's better at the end. - Warren Buffett.

L et's break down how this plays out in its entirety by looking at a completed pattern. Chart 1 from Chapter 4 remains unfinished because the two time periods haven't intersected, YET.

The second period, 2007 to 2021, travels faster than the first period, 1929 to 1966, creating a meeting point. To help illustrate, let's start with a completed smaller time horizon.

Observe this chart of the SP500 from March 2009 to Jan 26th, 2018.

Chart 6-1

A little over ¾ into the move (78.58% or 1 divided by 4.67) notice a brief dip down. Now let's start another chart there, moving 4.67 times faster than the first.

Chart 6-2

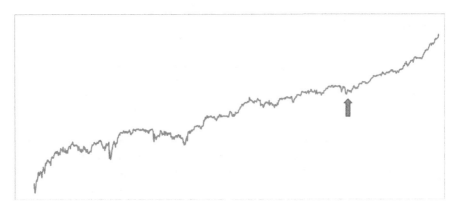

For a clearer picture, I have overlaid them on top of each other:

Chart 6-3

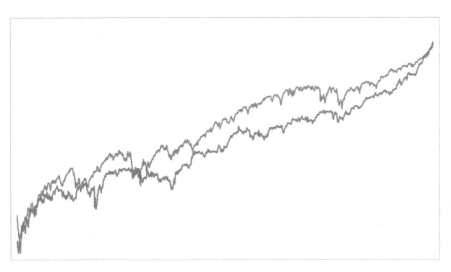

Now take the second chart, and repeat the process.

Chart 6-4

Now we have three charts. One starting in March 2009, one starting in February 2016, and one starting in September 2017. Chart 2 is 4.67 faster than chart 1. Chart 3 is 4.67 faster than Chart 2 and thus 21.8 times faster than Chart 1. All three end on Jan 26th, 2018. So, the first chart is approximately 9 years from start to finish. The second is 2 years. And the third is 4 months.

Notice on chart 3 I have placed another arrow. Now take the 3rd chart and repeat the process.

Chart 6-5

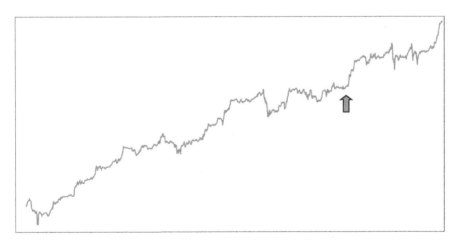

Now we have a 4th Chart starting in December 2017 and will move 4.67 times faster than Chart 3 and thus a little over 100 times Chart 1. This chart 4 will look like the others, only its duration is now 1 month. The entire pattern will once again play out, as these data points become the ultimate points of all the other periods; multifractal.

Notice the arrow on Chart 4. Now, perform this again. There will be a 5th period lasting only 1 week. This period goes 475 times faster than the period beginning in January of 2009 and will look like all the other periods. But it won't end there. There will be a 6th period lasting just longer than one day and will move at 4.67 times the speed of period 5 and 2200 times the speed of Chart 1.

Now we arrive at Chart 7.

Chart 6-7

This chart begins with an hour left and will mirror all the other charts as moves at over 10,000 times the speed of the first chart.

We have 7 different periods, all making a crescendo in unison. All related by the Feigenbaum constant.

Chart 7 also has an arrow. So you guessed it, this keeps going. By the time we reach chart 8, things move so fast, we have few data points, yet the pattern holds.

Chart 6-8

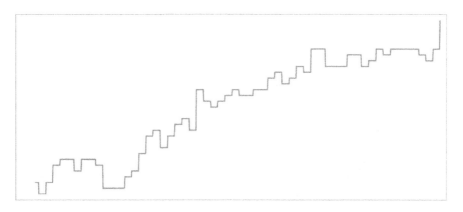

Upon completion on January 26th, 2018, a crash will ensue, wiping out the gains of most of the periods except the largest ones.

The crash performs like an avalanche. It takes down the excess snow, but the base level remains, and the mountain stays intact. FYI, avalanches are complex systems governed by these same rules.

Look at what happened after January 26th:

Chart 6-9

This break in price also contained a large jump in volatility. Think of it like a waterfall before it goes over the edge. The risk profile changes fast.

Now let's get back to our 1966 vs 2021 analogy. Hopefully, you have a better understanding of what I meant by not finished yet.

Imagine looking at the above series of charts before we had arrived on Jan 26th, 2018. Consider after Charts 2 and 3 were well underway, but before Charts 4 through 8 had arrived. I.e. The pattern had established itself enough to create a series of projected charts, but none had reached the terminal point. Now execute this on a longer-term basis and you have Chart 1 from Chapter 5. Take a minute and let this sink in.

IF the dynamics at play in the 2018 series of charts can scale to a larger period, THEN, we sit in a superb seat to witness all this play out on a bigger scale. I will show in the later chapters why I will back up this assertion.

I have searched long and hard for other people performing similar studies in the stock market to help me better understand this process. And I have yet to find anyone putting it together like the above. Didier Sornette has come the closest in his book "Why Stock Markets Crash."

Mr. Sornette is a professor of both Physics and Earth Sciences. In his work, he shows how to generate a critical point in a complex system. This provides a forecast for timing the peak and then crash. He accomplishes this by measuring the increasing interim peak intervals. With the 2009-2018 move, this value would have been 4.67.

He allows for each movement to have an independent variable; the move will create the variable. He claims you can predict the behavior once the acceleration has started. Thus, you scan for bubbles, then once formed, you forecast when they will end and come crashing down. He claims this holds for earthquakes, avalanches, and stock prices. I'll talk more about this in Chapter 13.

I take this further and claim the market's invariant structure leads to always behaving within the bubble/crash cycle. It becomes a question of scale.

We live within a bubble, within bubbles. Recall wishing wells, within wishing wells.

The modern technological revolution operates as one giant bubble. The roaring 20s or the dot.com boom — both followed by crashes — rest within a much larger bubble.

I claim this gigantic bubble has progressed far enough to produce an accurate prediction about when it will climax. Turns out it is 2052.

Where did the forecast come from? Let's look.

Chapter 7

Bulls and Bears Everywhere.

Is all that we see or seem
But a dream within a dream? - Edgar Allen Poe.

L et's go back and inspect the 1932 to 1966 vs 2009 to 2021 comparison from Chapter 4. This snapshot captures only a piece of the entire scale it's operating in. Now let's take what we did with January 2018, apply the logic to this larger scale. We will take the 1932 to 2021 data and go back further and add a few more layers.

The financial revolution started in 1600 when the Dutch and East India Companies formed. These companies emerge as the first stocks I have found data on. So let's start here, looking at 400 plus years. After parsing out the data, we discover the following.

First, an overall pattern and trend presents itself. Observe the following 'bubble' tops and the respective year of the high. I'm including the new technology associated with the bubble and the years between the consecutive tops:

Table 7-1

-The South Seas and Mississippi Co. - 1720 The sailboat/pigeon

-The U.S. railway mania - 1853 The train/telegraph 133 yrs

-The roaring twenties - 1929 The automobile/radio 76 yrs

-The gold and silver bubble - 1980 The airplane/t.v. 51 yrs

-The housing bubble - 2007 The computer/internet 27 yrs

- The currently forming bubble - 2025 The smartphone/social media 17 yrs.

The time intervals accelerate as the flow of goods and information speeds up. It doesn't take rocket science to discover a crescendo building. I.e. at some point, they will cascade on top of each other. Also, the speed of change will become so rapid, we might not even fathom its future speed.

If you told someone from the 1720s, the boats and canals they were building would set the stage for rockets, electricity, quantum computers, biotechnology and smartphones, they wouldn't have understood your musings.

Now recall the fractal or self-similar structure of the scale-invariant stock market. Thus, what is unfolding also unfolds on adjoining scales.

Therefore, **a major message of the market applicable to almost everyone alive today is: a minimum of a 400-year boom-bust cycle will form a top in 2052, then bust on at least this scale.**

The 9-year pattern I laid out in Chapter 4 repeats the process on a 400-year scale. Take a minute; let that set in…

The move, within the move, ending in January 2018, reiterates itself on a 400 years scale. And the mind-blowing part becomes in realizing all these moves have a mathematical relationship. The small ones on the 9-year scale, and the bigger ones on the 400-year scale, express each other. Mike drops.

For students of the markets, you might ask why didn't I mention other tops like 1937 and 1987? Well, from this unfolding, they were moves of a different scale than the primary ones listed in Table 1. They mirror the Jan 2018 top. They mathematically relate but reside on a smaller scale.

Boom and busts, including parabolic gains and ensuing crashes, happen all over the place on various scales.

A day trader sees mini ones frequently. And believe me, when you're trading in a short time frame using leverage, a one percent move coming out of "nowhere," feels the same as 1987 felt to any institution or investor.

Notice this move in the Swiss Franc during 2015. Currency markets are 'controlled' by the banking system and appear relatively stable. They are so stable, some players leverage their portfolios close to 100 times in these markets. They seek to capture one "pip," and do it with huge leverage. Typically, this works out well. Post $1000 in a trading account. Then leverage 100 to 1 and buy $100,000 worth of a currency, and make one $10 tick. With 250 work days in a year, repeat this once a day and make $2500 a year on your $1000.

Sounds awesome. And day in and day out it works. Then you get this:

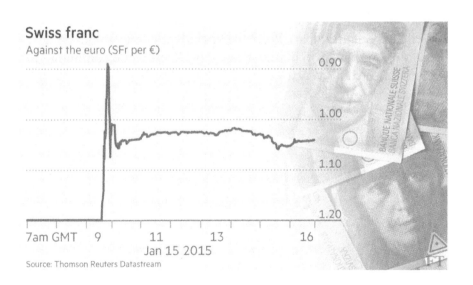

Swiss franc
Against the euro (SFr per €)

Source: Thomson Reuters Datastream

This is an astounding move for how stable a currency is. Your $1000 wiped out multiple times over. This is one heck of a fat-tail.

If you're prepared for it, and your position size aligns with your scale, then you will generate a great deal of money. If you're not ready for it, and you're over-committed, prepare for removal from the game. On a personal note, I have first-hand experience with both.

So how do we stay in the game for the next 30 years? Behold what the stock market divines.

-The upward marching trend from the last 400 years will continue, and head much higher than many people imagine.

-Get ready for major technological advances.

- Many jobs will go extinct, and multiple new industries will unfold.

- Epigenetic changes will speed up. We won't even recognize ourselves 30 years from now.

- The optimists have the edge.

And what about after that? Well, the apocalyptic folks might have their turn? For now, I'm putting that on the shelf while continuing to examine the next 30 years.

Chapter 8

Buckle Up, Times Speeding Up.

"Well, in our country," said Alice, still panting a little, *"you'd generally get to somewhere else—if you run very fast for a long time, as we've been doing."*
"A slow sort of country!" said the Queen. *"Now, here, you see, it takes all the running you can do, to keep in the same place. If you want to get somewhere else, you must run at least twice as fast as that!"* - "Through the Looking Glass." - Lewis Carroll.

W e awake as the first generations to witness more than one complete market cycle on the time scale I presented. Over the next few decades, we will witness many entire cycles. It's a scary yet exciting time. Scary, if you are about to lose your job from computer automation. Exciting, because of the exponential growth opportunities.

Building canals and sailing around the world improved the way people and trade moved versus the horse. When Columbus set sail in 1492, his venture was risky and unknown. 228 years later, the educated class in Europe got swept up with the rapid fortunes of the South Seas and Mississippi shipping companies. Sailing around the world was no longer considered a risky endeavor. It's now viewed as a sure thing and an easy way to get rich. Welcome to the top of the boat bubble.

Guess what comes next. The stocks came crashing down, wiping out the sure things. Sir Isaac Newton gave us calculus and the laws of gravity but was perplexed by the motion of these stock movements.

He could predict the motion of the planets, but he didn't yet have the laws of complexity to help him predict the behavior of the boat bubble stocks. A quick Google of the topic. We get talk of a two-year steep rise, and then a crash.

But I visualize this as the top of a 200-year move, followed by a 75-year crash. To use a metaphor from earlier, a leaf and the tree.

Look at these two charts. The first is the South Seas Trading Co. stock price from 1719 to 1722. The leaf.

Chart 8-1

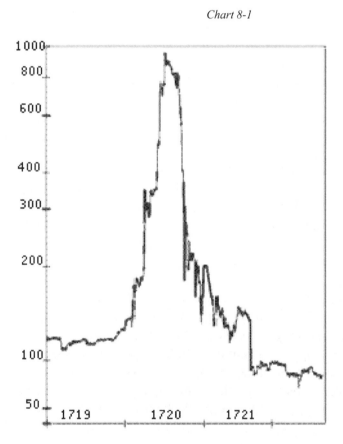

The second is the East India Trading Co. from 1602-1795. The tree.

Chart 8-2

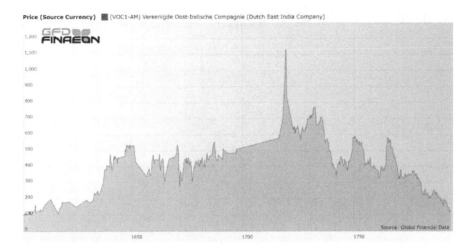

Price (Source Currency) ▉ (VOC1-AM) Vereenigde Oost-Indische Compagnie (Dutch East India Company)

This second chart provides a more accurate portrait of the entire movement.

One equals 3 years, the other 193 years. The top of the second chart coincides with the top in the first. It is the top of the boat bubble.

From the time of Columbus until the boat bubble topped, reached over two centuries. Imagine the massive undertaking to build ships, canals, and waterways from scratch. Especially without the help of electricity or steam and combustion engines. But build them we did. Things moved slowly and took a long time.

Cities sprang up in ports around the world, as goods and services moved at the speed of the boat rather than the speed of the horse. After the boat bubbles burst, we went to work with the newly created productivity. The boom and bust cycle facilitates the integration of its creation.

I'm going to jump ahead and say something about the internet bubble ending in 2000.

Here is a chart of the Nasdaq during this period.

Chart 8-3

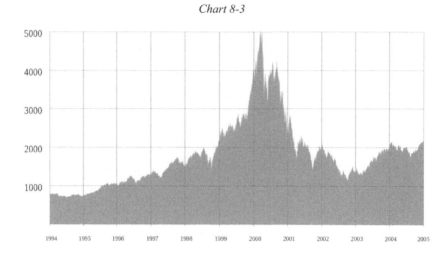

This bubble carries with it a negative connotation. Words like "irrational," and "excess speculation," get attributed to this period. But I would argue it's how it all works.

The internet came into being with the bubble. Without the bubble, it doesn't get built. It's a reflexive process.

I jumped ahead to help frame the boom-bust of the boat bubble. It too was a reflexive process, creating the backbone of the industrial revolution. After the boat bubble burst, a new network of cities emerged. This lays the foundation for the next boom-bust cycle. The start of the industrial revolution, and with it, the railroad.

Here we notice things speeding up. What took two centuries to build happens in half the time. But still a multi-generational cycle. From the time of the first engines, until the mania of 1853, was still longer than a generation. The vast productivity gains, once again, don't come until after the bubble has formed and busted. The full cycle unfolds in 133 years.

There were many booms and busts during this time, all at the speed and flexibility of the train. — They were cycles within the larger cycle of building the railroads.

Once again, after the tracks get laid, and the robber barons have made their fortunes, we have a network in place setting the stage for the next cycle; the automobile.

When the automobile arrives on the scene, the full cycle plays out yet again. This time, in 72 years.

For the first time, a well-timed birth could witness the complete cycle. But similarities would abound. Every cycle creates its relative billionaires at the forefront of pushing the wave down its path. It also wipes out the latecomers and easy money crowd. It also builds the foundation for the next wave. Henry Ford and the auto will now give way to Howard Hughes and the airplane.

Once again, the titans amassed new fortunes as technology, trade, and information all speed up. This time, from start to finish, in 51 years.

We have already touched on the 1929 to 1966 period. This isn't the full cycle. This cycle will end with the mania of the gold and silver bubble bursting in 1980.

Here lies an opportune time to introduce a second pattern to the entire boom-bust cycle presented in chapter 7. I call this second pattern, the "west coast" and "east coast" bubbles.

The boom-bust pattern happens in two prominent waves. The initial wave invents and establishes the new technology. The second wave occurs from all the recent financial productivity, hitting the economy from the modern improvement. I coined it the west coast and east coast because, during the last few cycles, the ground zero of the bubbles contain a different center.

The new technologies come out of companies having the 'story' and the 'vision' of the new frontier. The technology goes from an idea to an invention, to a risky proposition, and becomes such an awesome story it's easy money.

The wave of enthusiasm helps the story become a reality; it builds the reality of the vision. But the pattern repeats, and it eventually crashes back to earth. Then, amid the dust, a second bubble emerges from all the monetary gains from the new technology.

The first story wave has burst, yet productivity ensues. The silicon valley or west coast story- be it the halcyon stocks of the 60s or the dot.coms of the late nineties or the FAANG stocks of today - digest the hype, and crash from the lofty heights. But they leave fantastic productivity gains, creating massive new wealth in the total economy. This new productivity makes its way to the banking system and creates a subsequent east coast bubble. I.e. Wall Street.

The first wave is a story wave, and the second is a monetary phenomenon.

Now we can determine where some of those other significant moves fit in the picture. Observe the east coast move and the date of its peak, and the west coast move and the date of its peak:

Table 8-1

Tulip Mania 1637 and South Seas 1720

Panic of 1796 and U.S. Railroads 1853

Copper Corner 1907 and Roaring Twenties 1929

Halcyon period 1966 and the Gold Silver 1980

Dot.com 2000 and Real Estate 2007

FAANG 2021 and yet to be named 2025

Market timers rejoice because your time in the cycle arrives. Your return on investment from this book pays off right here. I'm confident you will receive your money's worth. Along with revenge from the passive allocators and the "never try to time the market" crowd.

Here lies the market script for the next few years. Notice the similarities to Chapter 4. Now it's multifractal.

2021 to 2024 will look like 1653 to 1690

2021 to 2024 will also appear similar to 1815 to 1836

2021 to 2024 will also appear similar to 1909 to 1922

2021 to 2024 will also appear similar to 1966 to 1974 (see chapter 4)

2021 to 2024 will also appear similar to 2000 to 2004

All these periods appear similar, except they are speeding up.

Now, just like there is a duality of the east coast, west coast within the cycle, every full cycle includes an alternating duality as well.

This materializes as an alternating inflation or deflation cycle. The reason I showed the 1928 to 1966 comparison in Chapter 4, rather than looking at the 1982 to 2000 comparison, rests in this second duality. Even though the price movement is similar — all these periods have over 90% correlation — the dynamics were more like 1929 to 1966 than 1982 to 2000.

Comparisons are showing up in the news, with the dot.com bubble of 2000 and today's cryptocurrencies. And it's obvious to fathom why.

In January 2021 Mark Cuban, the dot.com internet billionaire and Shark Tank host, had this to say: "Watching the cryptos trade, it's EXACTLY like the internet stock bubble. EXACTLY. I think BTC, ETH, a few others will be analogous to those that were built during the dotcom era, survived the bubble bursting and thrived... many won't."

Well, Mr. Cuban should know, he made billions on the internet bubble and was as close to it as anyone. And if you look at this chart, you'll see why he feels this way.

Chart 8-4

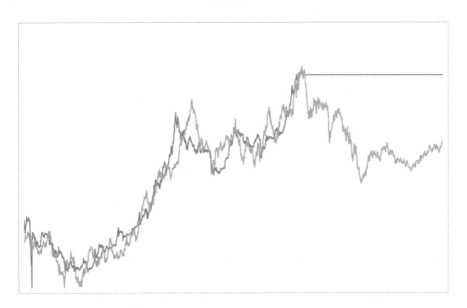

This is a chart of eight years of Bitcoin price from 2013 to 2021. Then Micron Technologies from 1988 until its top in 2000, then the subsequent fall. I think Micron is an excellent analogy for Bitcoin. DRAMS were labeled as the oil of the technology age by the company's original backer, billionaire J. R. Simplot. And cryptos will probably be the oil for the internet of things. Once again, fractals are stronger than analogs, as Bitcoin is moving faster than Micron Technologies. But the movement is striking. They are so tightly correlated, 97%, one has to strain to see two different price series.

So while similarities remain abundant between 2000 and today, the fundamentals of the next few years will appear more like 1966 to 1974 because of the inflation/deflation rotation.

So recapping. We have boom-bust; we have east coast-west coast, and we have inflation/deflation. Three-dimensional yin and yang. Being over 400 years into this big bowl, it has played out far enough to see it laid out in front of us.

DNA gives geneticists data for evolutionary theory. The Grand Canyon provides geologists the information for their geologic timelines. The cosmic microwave background confirms the physicist's big bang theory. Ice core samples preserved records for climate scientists to provide a global climate theory. The stock market now possesses sufficient data for an alternative theory for investors, economists, sociologists, futurists, eschatology, and think tanks.

And the theory says to get ready for some action. Because in a few short years, an entire wall street or east coast bubble will appear and crescendo like 1722, 1853, 1929, 1980, and 2007. Followed by a buying opportunity of a lifetime. This buying opportunity will look like 2009, 1982, 1932, 1860, and 1790.

But don't put your popcorn away yet! Because what took from 1600 to 1790, then from 1860 to 1929, then from 1932 to 1980, and then from 1982 to 2007 and again from 2009 to 2025, will happen from 2026 to 2035. Take a minute and let that sink in.

But don't take too long, because it will all play out yet again from 2036 to 2043. The complete cycle has gone from 190 years to 79 years to 48 years down to the 25 years it took from 1982 until 2007; the last completed cycle. The current cycle ends in 2025. Taking 16 years to accomplish what took 190 years a few centuries ago. And then it will all transpire again in 9 years.

Yes. A crash, a west coast bull market, digestion of the new technology, then a full-fledged east coast manic bull market followed again by a crash! All in 9 years. Then you guessed it. Again in 6, and then in 4, all the way down into super fast cycles putting an eye on the capstone in 2052.

You say — Impossible! The market will anticipate it and the pattern will go away. — I would say, don't bet on it. History and attractors say otherwise. It's how evolution marches forward. It's how the network of novelty, information, and complexification transpire. Physics has its law of thermodynamics or decay, and complexity has its power law of progress. Yin and Yang, decay and growth.

Chapter 9

It's not Just the Market

Deja vu all over again. - Yogi Berra.

When we wake up in the morning we're already cycling through personal boom-bust crescendos. On a small scale, it's a sugar rush, and then a sugar crash happening many times within the day. Then, on a bigger scale, there is the daily cycle of being awake, then falling asleep.

Notice the whole pattern, with the crescendo of the top, in the lovemaking cycle with a partner. Nothing happens for days, then it starts to build. Then a crescendo, followed by a crash.

Now push the time scale out further. We carry on in regular weeks, for weeks on end. Then we bring the family to Disney World. The pressure and intrigue build as the trip approaches. Then we climax into a week of over excitement, over stimulus, and overspending. We then experience a crash (we need a vacation from vacation), then we go back to normal weeks.

Goethe penned, "Everything phenomenal is metaphorical." The pattern is right there in Disney's logo; they understand their place in the cycle. Notice how the two sides of the castle aren't symmetrical. The left side moves up in waves as it crests into the top. Then the right side crashes as it falls faster than it rises. The star shows the arrow of time.

Disney's castle is the capstone of the cycle with our family.

But we digress. Let's continue lengthening our time scale.

On the next scale up, we build our families, then crash into a midlife crisis.

On the next scale up, we build our entire lives and then crash into death, leaving the next generation to do the same.

Like a kundalini serpent or the Hippocratic logo, this pattern once again has a Yin and Yang.

Caffeine or sugar high and crash, then a complete meal high and crash. We have REM sleep and deep sleep. An emotional crescendo with our partner one cycle, then a physical one the next time. Disney World with the family, then Viva Las Vegas the next time without them. An external midlife crisis, with fast cars or divorces. Then an internal midlife crisis with existential angst and depression.

It's frightening how predictable our lives have become. Ask Google and Facebook, they will tell you.

But let's circle back to the market with its vast amounts of data, enabling forecasts. And it predicts a the bigger scale is coming. It will play out. The attractor exists, pulling the market towards it. The only thing stopping it would be a larger attractor coming along. Currently, it would need something massive. Beyond anything, we have experienced in recorded history.

To better illustrate, let's look at hurricanes again. Imagine a hurricane plowing through the Gulf of Mexico. Let's name it a Category 5, making it strong. Our supercomputers can model this with surprising accuracy. As a Cat 5, almost nothing will stop this. Its path is set in stone. All the inputs are well-established. Therefore, the models will be accurate. But, let's say, an asteroid is heading straight for the earth and set to hit the Gulf of Mexico any moment. This asteroid will alter the hurricane and its projected path.

A bigger complex process will supersede the smaller process. A larger attractor will displace the smaller one. Without the asteroid, the hurricane will proceed. Upending every smaller attractor in its path.

Without an "asteroid," the market will proceed. So for safety's sake, let's go hunt for some "asteroids."

Let's begin by looking at bigger time scales than the last 400 years. We want to determine if we find any larger attractors sitting behind this one.

Chapter 10

The Bigger Picture.

When the ebbing tide retreats
Along the rocky shoreline
It leaves a trail of tidal pools
In a short-lived galaxy
Each microcosmic planet
A complete society

A simple kind mirror
To reflect upon our own
All the busy little creatures
Chasing out their destinies
Living in their pools
They soon forget about the sea... "Natural Science." - Neil Peart.

T he consensus view of our history reads something like this. The universe, as we currently understand it, burst on the scene 13.6 billion years ago.

And God said, "Let there be light," and there was light. God saw that the light was good, and he separated the light from the darkness. - Genesis, Chapter 1 verse 3-4.

Conjecturing about what was going on before this, or what may or may not lie outside of this, contains one of the biggest unanswered questions we have. But for now, we will put this aside, because we need to start somewhere. What do we learn if we start 13.6 billion years ago?

After the initial expansion, not much happened for billions of years. Time meandered. The earliest stars formed about 11 billion years ago. Estimates for the formation of our Milky Way stand at 8.8 billion years ago. A billion years boggles the mind of a human with an average lifespan of fewer than 100 years. It's over 14 million lifetimes. It's over 100,000 times longer than all of recorded history. It's over 3000 times longer than all Homo sapiens. It's 1 with 9 zeros. 1,000,000,000.

Another few billion years and our solar system formed 4.57 billion years ago. Already we perceive the boom-bust cycle. It's an enormous scale. Primordial gas "collapses," creating massive bulbs that combine and "complexify," creating galaxies. The smaller groups "fall into" larger ones, creating a bigger one with new stars and gases. This "complexification process" creates clusters, superclusters, voids, and filaments. Hmm. Yin and Yang. Boom and Bust. Novelty and Decay.

Right now, the nearest galaxy to the Milky Way is Andromeda. These two galaxies seem destined to collide about 4.5 billion years from now. We will detect the first effects approximately 3.5 billion years from now. What powerful bowls. Galaxies colliding epitomizes high drama. But it doesn't look like it will affect the next 30 years. So let's move closer to home. Our solar system.

Our solar system is chaotic and thus only predictable in the short term. We set calendars and clocks down to the millisecond and predict solar eclipses and planetary motions. We can only conclude this for about 10 million years. Beyond that, the chaos beneath the surface could rear its head. But, while it's chaotic, it resides in a period of relative stability.

And like the hurricane and the asteroid, any miscalculation or change in its conditions could send our entire solar system spinning out of control.

Recall the butterfly effect. It applies to all chaotic systems, including our solar system. We want to believe it's like a ball on a string being spun around, but it's not. It's a nonlinear, chaotic system whirling through space and is only stable at the moment because it's established in its pattern. It wasn't always like this and will eventually dissipate like all complex systems.

It's possible some unknown minor condition in our interaction with the other celestial bodies, whirling around with us, could alter our orbit. It's also theoretically possible all humans could jump simultaneously and change the rotation of Jupiter ever so slightly and therefore change the rotation of all the planets. This one slight change could go exponentially and spin earth into the sun, or another planet, or out into interstellar space. We could be the butterfly in a hurricane in the cosmos. The awesome news for us, the odds of either of these possibilities, are paltry.

Supercomputers have modeled our solar system, and they predict earth has a 99% chance of staying in a similar orbital plane to the one it is in now until our Sun dies approximately 4.5 billion years from now. So 99% we don't have to bother about this for 4.5 billion years and a 1% chance we don't have to anguish about this for another 10 million years. These are gigantic bowls! The sun will cook us a billion years from now. So, we will probably have to fret about this before spinning out of control. A billion is still an immense number, so unless the life-extension folks get their act together, none of us will have to worry about this one either.

So let's continue to move closer and look at our home planet, Earth.

Around 3.2 billion years ago, life on Earth showed up. Simple life, but life. It's single cells and viruses, and it's all moving slow. Photosynthesis arrives and then takes about a billion years to create enough oxygen for the next stage of life to form. Multicellular life arrives and the succeeding layer of complexity forms. This additional layer of complexity brings with it a boom-bust cycle. This modern life sets off a cycle of snowball earth. This lasts another billion years. Earth battles periods covered in ice as it deals with the fresh development of multicellular life. Things become more interesting as we hit 541 million years ago with the Cambrian explosion and its myriad of new types of life.

From there to here it is hardly a smooth ride. The fossil and ice records show 5 major extinctions and over 16 minor ones. In total, 21 extinction events. Some quick math says 541 divided by 21 equals an extinction event every 26 million years. The last minor one was 7.5 million years ago. The last major one, the infamous dinosaur killer 66 million years ago. 251 million years ago, Earth experienced the largest extinction, terminating around 80% of every living thing on the planet.

These cycles are in the millions, so the odds of this happening in the next 30 years seem slim.

Where should we examine next? How about Humans? We sometimes appear a danger to ourselves, so let's review our timeline and determine what it shows.

Let's put aside Darwin or Genesis, or any specific school of thought. Rather than litigate the merits of the various ideologies, let's agree to use a framework for approximate dates of record.

Let's view markers of complexification. The first animals arrived 600 million years ago. The first Tetrapods were 390 million years ago. The first mammals were 210 million years ago. Primates came on the scene 66 million years ago. Catarrhine Monkeys arrive 31 million years ago. Great Apes 15.7 million, Hominins 6.3 million, then we make it to Homo at 3.4 million years ago. And 1.9 million years ago, we had Homo Erectus, and we envision our ancestors. So let's pause here and take a quick inventory.

Are things growing more complex? Sure seems that way. Each stage checks multiple boxes of greater organization, networking, and complexity.

Let's see if things are speeding up? A quick look at the distance between these periods produces the following table:

Table 10-1

- 210 million years

- 180 million years

- 144 million years

- 35 million years

- 15.3 million years

- 9.4 million years

- 2.9 million years

- 1.5 million years

Hmm. Looks like it. And it is building a crescendo. It won't be long until we run out of millions.

At this point in the story, we are still at 1.9 million years ago; a significant amount of time if we're looking at our stock portfolio. Yet, we have a clear implication. We have less than 2 million years left before we evolve into something more complex! The other options include flat-lining, like the alligator, shark, and turtle. Or we die off?

So recapping. We have gone from the Galactic Bowl, with its 4 billion year from now threat, to the Solar Bowl with its 1 billion year threat, to the Earth-size bowl of 26 million years. Then further down to the Homo scale of 1.9 million years. The bowls seem to becoming shorter and getting faster. The data points aren't many, but in a multifractal universe, these few points have a tremendous amount of impact and meaning. Let's drill down further.

Chapter 11

The Technology of Man

I had a dream
Oh, yeah
Crazy dream, uh-huh
Anything I wanted to know
Any place I needed to go
Hear my song
Yeah, people don't you listen now?
Sing along
Oh
You don't know what you're missing, now
Any little song that you know
Everything that's small has to grow
And it's gonna grow, push push, yeah… - "The Song Remains the
Same." - Jimmy Page and Robert Plant.

Technology applies knowledge or engineering to achieve a
purpose. DNA does this. Now, at this point in the story, things
become interesting. A human being has shown up. And
humans can manufacture their technology. And we manage it quicker
than the mutating genes.

Rather than limiting ourselves to genetic change, we create epigenetic
change. Nature encodes its changes in irreversible DNA. Man creates
changes generating changes! We code our technology in places other
than DNA. Let's explore the timeline of how things have progressed.

Picking back up with Homo Erectus's at 1.9 million years ago, our
first major technology involves fire. Before this, other animals
already devised tools and coordinated hunting. Both examples of

epigenetic technologies. But Erectus also controls fire. The consensus view of its timing, coalesces somewhere in the neighborhood of 1 million years ago.

Fire changes the game. With it, brain size grows and proto-language begins. This creates a logical notch in the complexification belt. Now with some simple math, we see 1.9 - 1.0 equals 900,000 years and our time continues speeding up and our window shrinks to under a million years.

As our brain size keeps growing, Homo Sapiens arrived on the scene approximately 300,000 years ago. And with this bigger brain, and its cerebral cortex, we get the next notch in the evolutionary belt. This progress falls to 600,000 years.

The cerebral cortex is a fascinating piece of technology. We have changed little in the computation power of our brains since its development. It took nature 600,000 years to develop this. A lengthy time by our standards, but smaller than the billion years to travel from a simple cell to a multi-cell. So 1,000,000,000 years, with 9 zeros, to have cells dividing and only 600,000, with 6 zeros, to improve our awesome brains. We have 86 billion cells in our brain and 16 billion cells in our cerebral cortex.

What did we accomplish with this cortex? Well around 250,000 years later, at approximately 50,000 years ago, we arrived at another fantastic game-changing epigenetic technology: Language.

Along the way from 1.9 million years ago to 50,000 years ago, many booms and busts occurred. Of the 12 known branches of the genus Homo, only 1 remains. Us, Sapiens.

Erectus terminated. The Neanderthal perished. Habilis and all his cousins ended. There were ice ages and warm periods. Minor asteroid strikes and volcano eruptions. By some accounts, Homo Sapiens came close to extinction. Our numbers may have been as low as 10,000 in 70,000 BC.

By 50,000 BC, our ancestors are a complex piece of technology. We move around multiple continents and speak modern languages. The first known form of media arrives; cave paintings.

Cave paintings have a direct, mathematical, fractal relationship with television and social media. As a fun fact, we now have gone from the big bang to cave paintings. We have closed the circle of moving backward from social media to the cave painting I outlined in Chapter 4.

"The keys to. Given! A way a lone a last a love along the riverrun, past Eve and Adam's, from swerve of shore to bend of bay, brings us by a commodius vicus of recirculation," — James Joyce.

The next piece of major technology arrives 40,000 years later; Agriculture. Complexification garners the next notch in the evolutionary belt.

We now arrive at the Agricultural Revolution, which happens around 10,000 BC, or 12,000 years ago. This coincides with the Holocene. The Earth has warmed up and humans learn how to plant crops and domesticate animals.

The next wave of technological advancements shows up in 3,300 BC with the Bronze Age and the invention of writing.

After the Bronze Age collapses near 1300 BC, we invent smelting and grammar and start the Iron Age.

Another crash followed with a game-changer; the invention of the wheel. Historians label this period Classical Antiquity. It lasts from 500 BC until 500 AD and the fall of the Roman empire.

Then we begin the Middle Ages. This ends near the invention of the printing press and the advent of the Modern Times.

We have now circled around to the point we backed our way into in Chapter 8.

How does our progression look? I'll list the times again between periods:

Table 11-1

- 900,000 years

- 600,000 years

- 250,000 years

- 40,000 years

- 10,000 years

- 6,700 years

- 2,000 years

- 800 years

- 1000 years

- 900 years

- 280 years

We marched from the galaxies, through the solar system, onto the planet, into life, then complex life, and now our ancestors. At every scale, we have further complexification and shorter and shorter time intervals. Coincidence? I doubt it. Data over-fitting? Possible.

We went fast and accepted subjective dates. We directed our aim towards hunting for bowls, rather than argue with history or the consensus dates.

During our march back, it sounds like 280 years remains the shortest duration we found. How might this enormous picture fit into our 30-year forecast? Let's delve further into the science.

Chapter 12

4.669201609...

Long you must suffer, knowing not what,
until suddenly out of spitefully chewed fruit
your suffering's taste comes forth to you.
Then you will love almost instantly what's tasted.
No one
will ever talk you out of it.

"Uncollected Poems." - Rainer Maria Rilke.

In high schools across America - where I grew up - algebra, geometry, trigonometry, biology, chemistry, and physics are part of the curriculum. Why not Chaos Theory?

Most of our surroundings in are nonlinear, yet this isn't something we study? Had we studied this in high school, maybe it wouldn't have taken me thirty years to discover the Feigenbaum constant?

Most people have heard of Pi and its value of 3.14. Many people are familiar with e and its value of 2.718. These are examples of irrational mathematical constants. But what about another irrational constant; Feigenbaum's 4.6692?

3.14 is fundamental to geometry, and 2.718 is fundamental to calculus, but 4.6692 is fundamental to the behavior of complex systems. And complex systems abound. So how has this gone unnoticed?

There are countless videos online about math. Topics like Fibonacci, prime numbers, etc are popular and well subscribed. A kids' math video, "Blippi visits the Ice Cream Truck," possesses over 200 million views on YouTube. Yet, there is solely one video with over 1 million views about Feigenbaum.

Veritasium is a YouTube channel by Derek Muller. He did a video about 4.6692 and his 6 million subscribers made it by far the most-watched video on the topic. If you haven't seen it, I recommend watching it. How has this number been around since 1975 and gathered so little attention?

In 1987, James Gleick made chaos theory cool with his famous book "Chaos." But it seems it has yet to hit the mainstream or high school.

How unfortunate; the material is fascinating. A high school student would find it engaging building fractal mountains, logistic maps, and bifurcation diagrams on their computers. And yet...

So let's talk about 4.6692 and why this number has huge implications for the study of the stock market. What is 4.6692?

Every chaotic system that includes a one-dimensional map with a single quadratic maximum will bifurcate at this rate. What the hell does that mean? Any chaotic system with something moving up and down and has a minimum and a maximum will settle into a state (choose an attractor) at the same ratio as the other choices. Let's simplify further.

Any complex system, where the choice is up or down, will have strange attractors. And those attractors relate mathematically at approximately the same ratio; always.

Logistic maps are an excellent way to visualize this. If you're not familiar with one, check this out:

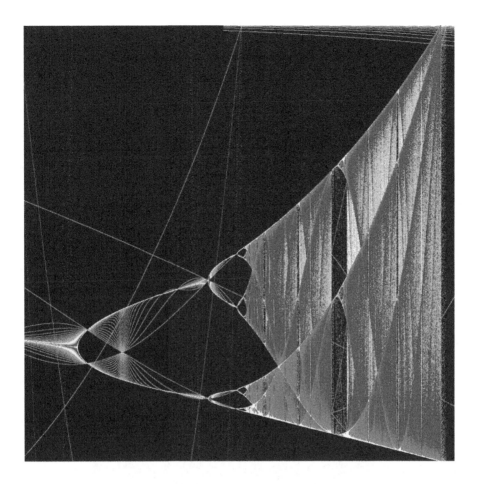

What is going on here? Well, this is the "road to chaos."

The bifurcations, on the left side of the image, are simple and stable. Initially, simply two bowls to choose from. Then 4 bowls. Then 8 bowls. Then 16... etc, etc. Eventually, the choice of bowls is a mess.

Imagine it like a pachinko board.

In pachinko, the ball only allows two options, right or left, as it works its way down the board. But the overall outcome has many paths towards the bottom. The logistic map is akin to a **cascading** pachinko board. With the game, each node contains the same ratio. 1 to 1. In the logistic map, each node carries the same ratios as well. 4.66692.

4.6692 is the ratio between each of these choices as we move down the road to chaos. This is a fractal. Any smaller branches look like the entire image. And, at each of these many, many, many branches, the ratio between them is always near 4.6692. We call this universality.

Pachinko has universality. It's a simple game. We recognize its universality. As difficult as it seems to comprehend, complex systems also contain universality.

Now let me remind you, every system of this type, conforms to this constant. We still don't know where this number comes from. I'll speculate in Chapter 25, but knowing it or not, our January 2018 crescendo from Chapter 6, illustrates its alive and well in the stock market.

When we march the math up a scale, we find it again. So, not only is it present, it might be the dominant force.

Why am I jumping to this conclusion? Because of power laws. What are power laws? Let's look.

Chapter 13

Power Laws

It's all just the same thing over and over; we can't help ourselves. And you and I can't control it or stop it, or even slow it, or even ever-so-slightly alter it. We just react. And we make a lot of money if we get it right. And we get left by the side of the road if we get it wrong. And there have always been and there always will be the same percentage of winners and losers, happy fuckers and sad suckers, fat cats and starving dogs in this world. Yeah, there may be more of us today than there's ever been. But the percentages-they stay exactly the same.

John Tuld. Played by Jeremy Irons in the movie "Margin Call."

I would guess, somewhere in the backroom of a substantial pool of capital lies a program like my analysis. It's improbable I'm the first to identify this pattern? Yet, I have searched for others on the same path and to date have found none. As I have already mentioned in chapter 6, the closest thing I've found was "The Log-Periodic Power Law Singularity" introduced by Didier Sornette in his book "Why Markets Crash." In a recent research paper with his colleagues, he sums it up as follows:

Begin quote: Based on the analyses of many historical bubbles, the studies have documented that there are transient regimes during which the price growth rate (return) grows itself, which translates into a super-exponential time dynamics. Such a pro cyclical process involves positive feedback, which can be of many types, such as option hedging, portfolio insurance strategies, margin requirements, as well as the imitation and herding behavior in psychology. These mechanisms tend to increase and accelerate the deviation from an equilibrium. The resulting super-exponential price trajectories are inherently unsustainable and often burst as crashes or strong corrections. In a nutshell, the existence of a transient faster-than-exponential price growth can be taken as a signature of bubbles. The advantage of this definition of a bubble is that it does not rely on the estimation of what is a fundamental value, which is poorly known as mentioned above. The Log-Periodic Power Law Singularity (LPPLS) model has been proposed as a simple generic parameterisation to capture such super-exponential behavior, which is inspired from physics (and is sometimes referred to as part of econophysics). This model takes into account that positive feedbacks generically lead to finite-time singularities. Moreover, it includes log-periodic oscillations decorated by accelerating oscillations, which are the observable embodiment of the symmetry of discrete scale invariance. This generic log-periodicity accounts for the existence of a discrete hierarchy of group sizes and may also result from the interplay between nonlinear value investors and nonlinear trend followers, and the inertia between information flow and price discovery. In summary, the LPPLS model provides a convenient representation of financial bubbles. End quote.

I humbly suggest he doesn't take it far enough. He shows how a bubble in the stock market is governed by power laws. Yet by their nature, power laws scale. They are fractal. Therefore, IF he uses research in physics models to prove bubble and crash behavior predict finite-time singularities, THEN it's inherent in the system, by nature of the embedded self-similarity in power laws, there would be bubbles and crashes within bubbles and crashes. Stated more simply: It's either not a power law, or it's happening at multiple scales. This is a feature of power laws!

So let's back up. What is a power law? A formal definition would be:

A power law is a functional relationship between two quantities, where a relative change in one quantity results in a proportional relative change in the other quantity, independent of the initial size of those quantities: one quantity varies as a power of another.

Understanding this concept has helped me reframe many situations beyond the markets. Allow me to elaborate.

In the above chapter quote, Jeremy Irons is describing the Pareto effect or fat tail distributions. i.e. a power law.

Nature builds networks and evolves with fat tails, not smooth distributions.

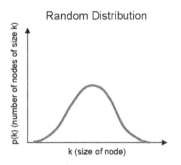

Random Distribution

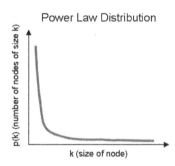

Power Law Distribution

In layperson's terms, it's the 80/20 rule. For many outcomes, roughly 80% of consequences come from 20% of the causes. The exact math looks more like the 78.6/21.4 rule (1 / 4.6692 = .2141), but that doesn't have the easy ring to it. The outcomes remain messy, therefore 80/20 works as a ball park rule.

Let's illustrate this with Mr. Iron's income distribution. 80% of the world's wealth is in roughly 20% of the people's hands. But it's fractal. Therefore, of those 20%, 80% of this wealth remains controlled by 20% of those. And so on.

We will do some simple 4th-grade math, and we notice .2 x .2 = 4%. Therefore, the wealth is further concentrated in only 4% of the population. But once again, the 80/20 rule applies to this group. Now we have .2 x .2 x .2 = .08%. We have arrived at what we refer to in our culture as "the 1 percenters."

But the concentration continues. Among the 1%, the 80/20 rule still applies. And therefore 80% of the one percent is owned by 20% of this group as well. And it holds all the way to the top.

Look no further than the last U.S. Presidential election. Senator Bernie Sanders is rich from almost any American's viewpoint. If we gave him the option to throw a number into a hat with every other American, and then draw a new number and trade monetary places with them, he would never put his number in the hat. Yet, compared to President Trump's financial net worth, he is a picker. If Mr. Sanders could put his number in a bowl with only the 600 Billionaires in the United States, he would do it.

Now, let's say President Trump is worth $3 billion. Who knows what the actual amount is, but for the sake of the argument, let's assume it is in the ballpark. Even at 3 billion, he too is a picker compared to Mayor Michael Bloomberg with a net worth of somewhere around $65 billion. There is a vast difference between $65 billion and $3 billion.

This is the 80/20 rule playing out to the top. The spread between these groups is a fat tail. There is an enormous gap between the average and the top at each level. This is a way of saying the system isn't fair. And guess what, it's not fair. This doesn't mean it's rigged or a vast conspiracy. It means evolution has found fat tails are a robust way to build networks of any kind. This includes income distribution and stock markets.

This feature of power laws is called scale invariance. This means the 80/20 rules are happening at every level. Let me repeat differently because it's important.

Fat-tails reside at every scale.

Fat tails rule in the market. And it is ingenious they do. IF markets were evenly distributed, THEN making money would be super easy and stock charts would look like straight lines. Any intelligent player would leverage to the exact optimum of the variability of the distribution. Game Over! Fat tails keep this from happening.

Charlie Munger -Warren Buffett's partner we met in Chapter 2- is much smarter and more accomplished than me, and he thinks "irrational" short-term traders are hazardous to the market. I disagree. They play a vital role in building a complex network. The system requires considerable sigma events. The Federal Reserve likes to think it can stop fat tails, but I would say there is a fat chance of that. The system would be dead without crashes and "irrationality." Fat-tails keep things robust and alive.

A powerful message of the market, that would help everyone better frame their own lives, would be to accept and appreciate fat tails. Put in simple terms, embrace the draw-downs. Celebrate both growth and decay. They are both parts of the system.

Also, while the system isn't fair, it's the same for those at the top. Fat tails keep the game moving. It's difficult for fortunes to be preserved. The ranks at the top change. Players come and go. It appears static, but it's anything but. There is a survivorship bias leading us to believe the power and wealth are ensconced and static. It is not. Fat tails see to it.

If you think your neighbor has it better than you, give it time. A fat tail will arrive. It's nature's way, and it's ingenious. Death provides the ultimate fat tail. And everyone will experience it. And death keeps the system robust.

Getting back to the market. If power laws are ruling the market, which I contend they are, then they will enable us to create an accurate stock market forecast like our weather forecasts. The 2018 top I presented in Chapter 6, is a real-time illustration of a power law in action in the market! Even better, the Feigenbaum constant governs it. If I communicate this effectively, it could change how we appreciate the world.

Further confirmation would come if we could tie it to a larger scale. And I accomplished this in Chapter 7.

Recall the feature of power laws that states,one quantity varies as a power of another. The small moves in the market reflect the large moves and visa versa. Therefore, **I predict we will have a stock market prediction on our news feeds as accurate as weather predictions.**

Chapter 14

The Stock Market Forecast

All truth passes through three stages. First, it is ridiculed. Second, it is violently opposed. Third, it is accepted as being self-evident. - Arthur Schopenhauer.

The 1973 book "A Random Walk down Wall Street" has sold over 1.5 million copies and is in its 12th edition. It laid out the framework for the "efficient market hypothesis". (EMT) This theory states oversized returns are not possible because the market is a discounting mechanism. I.e. any advantage or exploitable pattern gets arbitraged out by the players. The theory postulates for a short period you might find an edge in the market, but soon someone else will follow and the edge will revert to the mean results of the marketplace. This book claims a stock market forecast will never be possible. But the fat tails we looked at in Chapter 13, already illustrate the efficient market has holes in it.

Statisticians call the crash of 1987 a high sigma event. The move is somewhere between 6-20. It is so high it is difficult to measure it. So it was a 6-20 standard deviation move away from the average. Therefore, it should happen somewhere on the order of once in a million years to once in an incalculable amount. Literally. So clearly, someone using EMT has some explaining to do. This doesn't mean EMT can't be beneficial. However, it has limitations.

Newtonian physics gives us many answers to how physical objects behave, but it doesn't help us solve the wishing well problem. Newton himself understood this and had postulated about what is now understood as the butterfly effect. But Newton didn't have our

---

computers, and without supercomputers, these problems were out of reach.

Currently, we have the computing power to perform calculations of these complex systems. Already near the bifurcation points, excellent predictions are possible. The Prediction Company talks about how they were successful in doing this as early as 1991 by hooking up a bunch of sun micro-system computers to each other.

Given innumerable points are happening on many scales in the markets, we will have countless predictions with strong validity. It's only a matter of time until machine learning and AI figure it all out. Allow me an example of how this is already happening with another complex system, the weather.

Predicting the weather isn't perfect, but it is super helpful. We have come a long way from devising markings on the rocks to help us plan for the seasons.

Our ancestors were making these marks because they noticed the shadow from the sun would move across the rocks until it hit the same point every time and then started going in the opposite direction. And when this happened, the temperatures would move in the opposite direction. Also, the days would get longer or shorter depending on which way the shadow was now moving.

What they were doing was "predicting" the tilt and rotation of the Earth. Back then, we didn't even understand why this happened. We only knew the shadow of the sun moved predictably as we established the marks on the rocks. They had found a large, stable attractor.

Now with our supercomputers, we know the hour we will need an umbrella. And we understand the science behind why.

5000 years ago, it would have seemed like voodoo or magic to have the weather predictions we take for granted today. So I predict we will accept and use market predictions. And it will delight the supercomputers to oblige. If a supercomputer owner wants to call me, I'll be overjoyed to talk about the possibilities of how to bootstrap the process.

How could this be possible? If everyone knows the prediction, won't it be invalid? Absolutely not. Complexity isn't perfectly predictable. Like the weather, it contains variability. Recall they are strange attractors, not Newtonian ones. Option skews will look different from today, but they still will have some skew.

And if you are in the business of making markets in options using models from EMT and Black Scholes, you better be prepared to go out of business. The supercomputers will render your current models worthless. They will become invalid and a sure loser. A fat tail is on its way. Once again, if an options market maker wants to stay in business and doesn't understand the fat-tail on the horizon, call me.

But even a small amount of skew in a low-interest-rate environment would lead to many "random" return distributions. Machines and A.I. could "control" the market by this stage. And this prediction could even be self-reinforcing if A.I. makes the calls.

The bots could get in a reinforcing feedback loop of gradient ascent.

The machines wouldn't be limited to our linear-minded egos, and they would learn better than us and "go where the market wants to go." Which ironically could be part of the process of bringing the market there.

This would create a playing field where most market participants have semi-uniform results. Thus leaving the super quick AI's battling it out the way our market titans of yesteryear used to do it.

Don't think it could happen? Ask any "big swinging ****" on the floor of the exchange 20 years ago if they believed a computer was coming to take their job and do it way better than they do. They likely would have dismissed the idea as ridiculous. But this transpired.

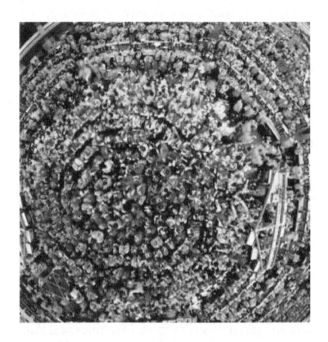

And just like the bid/offers are way too fast for any human to do by hand, as 2052 approaches, the movement will become too fast for any money managers. So, money managers, your job is a risk just like the options guys. See the picture of the floor? It's empty now, and this is your fate as well. So get ready.

The occupy Wall Street crowd can rejoice, because fat-tails will disrupt the entire industry just like everywhere else.

And like I already said, computers won't be stupid or arrogant enough to change nature's pattern. They will accept it, get on board, and be a part of the process of making it happen. It's nature's way of building novelty. And if we look around and are paying attention, we will see it is already happening. The stage is set.

Chapter 15

Mindgasm

Mindgasm (noun) - An exhilarating neurostorm of intense intellectual pleasure. Fully revelatory understanding of a certain topic. Involuntary contractions of brain muscles usually accompanied by the overwhelming sensation of truth proximity. Visionarism. State of awe. - Jason Silva.

Ok, let's take this one step further. I'm taking the cube root of the Feigenbaum constant, thus moving from a one space dimension to a three-space dimension. This accomplishes two critical elements. First, it more closely mirrors a finance chaotic attractor. Second, it backs us into a cascade of the east coast, west coast, and inflation/deflation rotation all the way down.

Think of the plate rotation game. This is where you attempt to rotate a plate 360 degrees without the food falling off. This requires spinning it twice.

One complete set of rotations gave us the 1929 to 1966 comparison with today. - Chart 1 from Chapter 4.

With two sets of two full rotations, we produce the following graph:

Chart 15-1

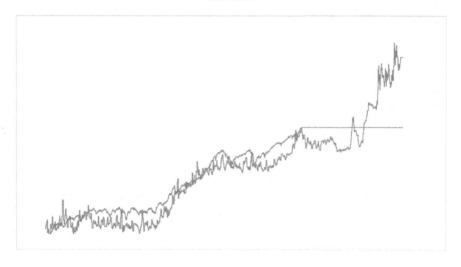

If this chart fails at creating a sense of amazement, then I haven't done an adequate job in my presentation.

Here lies part of the front cover of the book. The dark line captures 741 years of wheat prices from 1280 A.D. until May 2021. The gray line chronicles 68 years of the S&P 500 from 1953 until May 2021. The two periods have a 96% correlation. Currently, the gray line sits at the year 1815 relative to the past. And mirroring Chart 1 from Chapter 4, these two charts will also meet up in 2052.

I hope I didn't lose you. So I'll sum up.

Fifteen chapters get reduced to this:

The stock market is operating under a chaotic power-law with a ratio of ∜ 4.6692 and a critical time period of 2052.

Too simple? I doubt it.

Stephen Wolfram is a mathematician, physicist, and computer scientist. He was the youngest ever MacArthur Fellowship winner.

He claims in his book, "A New Kind of Science," "From an extremely simple model, we're able to reproduce special relativity, general relativity and the core results of quantum mechanics. He adds, simple programs are enough to capture the essence of almost any complex system."

What makes for a simple program?

-Its operation can be completely explained by a simple graphical illustration.

-It can be completely explained in a few sentences of human language.

Check and check. I have given my simple yet powerful argument in one sentence and one graph. And I assert the graph will continue. As many layers, confirm the conclusion.

Wheat multifractals itself. In theory, in 1815, we could have taken the price data of wheat from 1280 A.D. and created a forecast for the next 200 years. This was possible because we had 535 years of historical data.

This forecast would have brought us up to today and explained 80% of what transpired in wheat prices from 1815 until now. And by the time wheat finished its bull move of 1922 and 1973, the correlations for predicting the 2008 move were even higher.

Furthermore, the S&P 500 copies wheat by the same multifractals with itself.

Now it's just a matter of time until they finish what they have already started.

As impressive as the last chart is, it's not perfect. It's not 100% correlated. It is still messy. If it were 100% correlated, we would live in a deterministic universe.

So the market might have something to say about free will? If the S&P 500 was 96% explained by movements in the past, then the remaining 4% is:

A) random
B) not explained yet
C) the amount of free will in the system.

4% sounds small, but over time, it will eventually add up to sideswiping everyone. Fat-tails and lady luck keep things messy.

Chapter 16

Lady Luck

I found a four leaf clover
In my yard today
It had one leaf missing off it
But that was okay

Looking it over I could easily see
Four is only just one more than three
That's close enough for me
Must be my lucky day - "Slim Chance." - Todd Snider.

Before every football game, the referees flip a coin, determining who kicks off first. Somewhat of an oddity for the rules of a sport. Why not a tip-off like basketball? Or home teams like baseball? What's with the coin? Maybe it's a metaphor for the recognition that luck plays a role in the game?

Poker is the most recognized game in the world outside of video games. The World Series of Poker has the largest prize pool of any sporting event. Television viewership is high, and they play tournaments all around the world. To win a poker tournament, the player must possess skill and mastery of the game. But they also must have luck. It is impossible to win a poker tournament by skill alone. A player cannot skill their way to the top.

If we prefer to play a card game where skill reigns supreme, consider playing duplicate bridge. Duplicate bridge pales in popularity relative to poker? Maybe because people choose a game, anybody can beat anyone, and poker provides that. If we want a card game based on luck, then beggar thy neighbor might be more our style. The outcome is predetermined when the cards are dealt. Poker finds itself in the middle ground; not all skill and not all luck.

The question becomes, are the markets more like beggar thy neighbor, poker, or duplicate bridge?

The markets are not like beggar thy neighbor. We better know how to play. It turns out we can't skill our way to the top either. Fat tails prevent this from happening. Even though the market is predictable, winning at the stock market game still requires some luck. Luck shows up as *when* we receive a fat tail because we will get them. It's part of the system.

Warren Buffett's formula is pretty straightforward. It leans on a couple of simple elements. Find a stable cash flow. Buy the cash flow and try not to overpay. A third crucial tool for his success; let compounding do its thing. This one breaks the deal for most. It requires patience.

Compounding is impressive. At 50, Mr. Buffett was "only" worth 1 billion dollars. He started early in life, which helps if you're planning on letting compounding work for you. If he started at 10, it took him 40 years to grow the 1 in front of all those zeros. Today, 40 years later, he owns 100 billion. The first 40 years =1 billion. The following 40 years = 100 billion. - This doesn't include the 37 billion he has given away. Was he doing anything different? Not really. It is harder today than it was earlier because of the law of large numbers. Being big opens some doors, but it also closes many. Witness the power of compounding in action.

A key to compounding involves avoiding fat tails. Since we will have them, when they arrive matters.

Saloman Bros was a fat tail for Mr. Buffett. Had it come earlier in his career, without a doubt, he wouldn't be anywhere near as wealthy as he is today. Buffett also had some mistakes. US Airways and Dexter Shoe are the ones he mentions himself. But mistakes are part of the game, and if his money management is solid, there will still be plenty of capital left to compound.

Fat tails differ from mistakes. Saloman Bros was a huge moneymaker. Being a prime dealer for government securities is as close to a sure thing as you see. Thus, it had cash flow, the flow was stable, and it had a long shelf life. No mistakes buying this.

But Saloman Bros found itself in a scandal in 1991, brought on by a few players pressing their sure thing. Mr. Buffett's holding company was the largest shareholder. To Buffett's credit, he handled this situation with tremendous skill. However, had this event happened earlier in his lifetime, his entire net worth would be substantially different.

He could have done everything the same; bought a superb company at a reasonable price, then had a few rotten apples upend the whole apple cart. But this time, let's pretend it happened shortly after managing outside capital. At a minimum, it would have given him less capital to compound, and at a maximum, it might have kept him from attracting any capital to compound. Either way, his results would have been different, and the only change was when the fat tail occurred.

There are likely many Buffett would have, could have, should have's out there. Buffett holds the distinction of being the one who lucked his way to the top. This captures a survivorship bias in action. We know about Mr. Buffett because he holds the crown worth 100 billion dollars. Countless others may have been as adept investors, orators, and teachers as Buffett, but they had the unfortunate luck of having a fat tail early in their investment tournament life.

Citadel is a prosperous hedge fund. The owner, Ken Griffin, is the richest person in Illinois. He makes markets, and excellent market makers have dependable income streams. Their profit-and-loss curves look different from stock prices. By the last unconfirmed count, Citadel's leverage ratio stood at 7 to 1. Some simple math tells us if all his assets fell by 15%, it would wipe him out.

Clearly, he is doing something different from Mr. Buffett. Citadel can leverage higher because their returns are more stable. The smooth curve I talked about in Chapter 13 is working for him. He is on the way to owning everything. He has skilled his way into a ruler profit-and-loss curve, going straight and up. No curves here, right? Wrong.

Once again, fat tails lurk on the horizon. Growth curves that look like a ruler, often end abruptly. It doesn't imply a blowout like Long Term Capital Management. The earnings stream could merely go to zero overnight.

If the exchanges put a speed buffer on all incoming orders, every market maker relying on speed for their competitive edge would be out of business. All the overhead and intellectual capital put in place would become worthless in an instant. If this happens, game over.

A sizable transaction tax could produce the same. A rogue employee could accomplish the same. An A.I. supercomputer could perform the same. There is a fat tail out there, it just hasn't hit Ken Griffin. He has been lucky. He possesses extraordinary expertise, but he has also been lucky.

Other firms may have spent millions building high-speed networks only to have the exchange move where they located their servers. This firm got hit with a fat tail, so we don't read about their owner being the richest person in their state.

Switching gears, Ray Dalio is the billionaire founder Bridgewater Associates, the worlds largest hedge fund. He is also an author and blogger sharing his big picture views. He makes the assertion that America has reached its peak and that our system is set to to have it's fat tail moment as we lose our reserve currency status.

I bring up Mr. Dalio here because he has composed the following simplified chart to show what is about to happen to the worlds largest economic power. He claims our empire is at the top of the chart and heading down.

The Typical Big Cycle Behind Empires' Rises and Declines

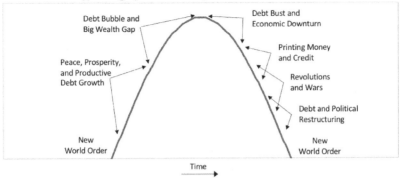

Debt Bubble and Big Wealth Gap

Debt Bust and Economic Downturn

Peace, Prosperity, and Productive Debt Growth

Printing Money and Credit

Revolutions and Wars

Debt and Political Restructuring

New World Order

New World Order

Time

How could America have a debt bust, revolution and war, political restructuring and a loss in its reserve currency status at the same time the stock market will ecstatically march to massive new highs into 2052?

Well either:

A) Mr Dalio's model is incorrect..
B) Mr. Dalio's model is prescient, but early.
C) My market model isn't a valid model.
D) The market will explode higher in nominal terms, but not in absolute terms. I.e. hyperinflation.
E) The U.S. economy will indeed collapse, and the market will march right through this fat tail, with an ecstatic ensuing phoenix.

I vote B or E.

Fat tails are like bad luck. After they happen, we think the sky is falling. But, like in Chicken Little, the overall system recovers and booms to new highs, confounding overly analytical thinking.

Recall we will have multiple major crashes along the way. However, the system will march higher and prevail.

I mention this here because I view events like this as part of the existing process. We might have a world war and countless other tragedies we have already witnessed in the last 400 years. And we will still march higher. As crazy as it sounds, a failed government or a world war isn't a bigger bowl than the scale we are in. These are "normal" events in a growing network. We might associate them with one of our many crashes, but they will be buying opportunities.

An asteroid is an outlier, a failed government is not. Look no further than Germany. It is a powerhouse on the world stage. It is the world's 4th largest economy. Its currency had a complete collapse in 1923 after WW1. And its government had a complete collapse after WW2. And look at them now. They have been lucky.

If the collapse had happened in their infancy, they would not have been so lucky. But, like Mr. Buffett, they were big enough to survive a late-stage fat-tail, and so too will the stock market.

When Mr. Griffin gets hit with a fat tail, he could easily survive it and eventually press higher. The financial crisis of 2008 worked as a mini fat-tail for Mr. Griffin. He is established, and therefore robust.

However, a new fat tail would halt his pace of owning the world. Because at the pace he is on, he would own the world if a fat tail never arrived.

Yin and Yang, skill, and luck. It's not a coincidence we call it lady luck. The lady implies the opposing force with the controlling male. It also acknowledges the chaos or uncertainty.

The predictive correlations laid out in this book, are powerful enough, if no one else had them, in theory, I would eventually own everything. But I'm giving these tools for the price of a book?

I also conform to these laws, therefore it is helpful to incorporate something Benoit Mandelbrot said about fractals into framing these type questions: *"Clouds are not spheres, mountains are not cones, coastlines are not circles, and bark is not smooth, nor does lightning travel in a straight line."*

Luck is part of the equation. It's nature's way. That's why we like poker and why we like a coin toss to start football games.

Chapter 17

Tying the Bow

The test of science is it's ability to predict. - Richard Feynman.

L et's sum up the 30-year stock market prediction.

As promised, I have shown the genesis and explained why it's relevant, valid, and timely.

I have meet the criteria for a valid prediction. It is specific. It has a theory. It is replicable. And, it has been stated in advance.

It may sound counterintuitive, and difficult to accept, but recall we predict the movement of our solar system and set our calendars very accurately and it too is a complex system.

The Lyapunov time is a measure of the system's limit of predictability. The solar systems Lyapunov time is long compared to a human life span. Therefore, we take it for granted. To accept my forecast, all we need to realize is that the Lyapunov time for the stock market is longer than generally recognized. Quants on wall street successfully chase the rocks in the river from Chapter 2. I am providing the map of the river.

So, difficult to accept or not, these dates are valid.

At the time of this publication, we find ourselves at the top of a west coast bubble. Mirroring 1372, 1653, 1815, 1906, 1966 and 2000.

Chart 17-1

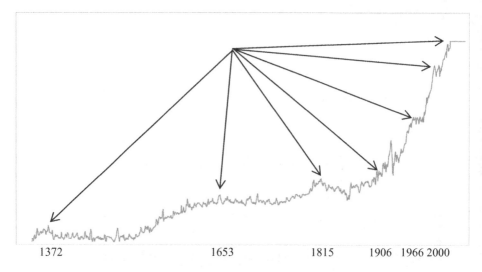

| 1372 | 1653 | 1815 | 1906 1966 2000 |

The market will rotate leadership, and trend lower on a nominal basis into late 2024. Then an east coast bubble will ensue and peak in 2026 as it mirrors 1492, 1722, 1853, 1929, 1980 and 2007.

We will have a crash in 2026. Then it will be time to return to buy and hold, until the next west coast bubble peaks again in 2034.

This will repeat at faster and faster intervals of $\sqrt[3]{}$ **4.6692,** building a crescendo into 2052.

Each period will move faster than the others, as they all move in unison. There will be an element of spin, as they cycle through inflation and deflation.

Each move will have nuance and novelty and will reach a critical point for its scale. So, we will be able to track the progress at multiple scales as we progress. For anyone interested, I will monitor this on my website. www.ecstaticstocks.com

This will transpire unless something **MUCH** larger comes along and supersedes this attractor.

This pattern is at work on the quantum level and the galactic level. This is the scale of the human level.

Fight this pattern at your peril, or climb on board for the ride. Remember to "go where the market wants to go." "The trend is your friend." For the next 30 years, the trend is up.

Part 2

On the Shoulders of Giants

Every artist is a cannibal, every poet is a thief. - The Fly - Bono.

In part two, I provide a synopsis of a few thinkers whose work echoes similar themes, albeit from their respective fields. I will stick to the primary bullet points. Each of these individuals has ideas filling more than a book, so attempting to fit it in a brief chapter holds challenges. These themes come from different backgrounds, so hopefully at least one of these thinkers stems from a field to which you, the reader, relate.

Chapter 18

Geoffrey West

I think the next century will be the century of complexity. - Stephan Hawking.

G eoffrey West has won the distinction of Time magazine's 100 most influential people. He graduated with a degree in physics from Cambridge and was president of the Santa Fe Institute.

This Institute does non-profit research in CAS. The group comprises members who have contributed to the fields of chaos theory, genetic algorithms, complexity economics, and systems biology among others.

In his work, he discusses a universal time which is emergent as the network gets built. This time is fractal. He further says,complex systems display an underlying simplicity.

Sounds like the exact message of the market.

He wrote a book titled "Scale." Here is a quote of the book's purpose. "A major intent is to show that underlying the extraordinary complexity, diversity, and apparent messiness of the world lies a surprising unity and simplicity when viewed through the lens of scale."

He is a scientist who examines scale in organisms, cities, economies, and companies. This graph provides an example of scale in organisms:

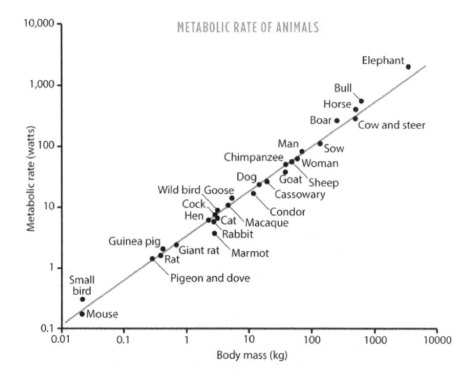

METABOLIC RATE OF ANIMALS

Mr. West theorizes we live in an exponentially expanding socioeconomic universe. This expansion isn't arbitrary; it obeys some simple underlying laws and contains universality. These laws make the system scalable, predictable, and resilient. Yet, it is also unsustainable.

It grows and decays. It evolves, then has entropy. It adapts, then repairs. It awakens, then sleeps. (In market speak it booms and busts) As the network grows, so grows its complexity and intelligence. And all networks get built as fractals and grow exponentially and hierarchical. This exponential growth climaxes in a singularity, and then the system crashes. After the crash, we establish a new exponential curve with its singularity. And so on, and so on, and so on. Each of these curves gets quicker and quicker.

He states it like this. "Socioeconomic time is the time we feel. It is the real time. It is the time we operate under. And where we are now is that we are on a treadmill that keeps building up to a point that we must jump off to a different treadmill that is going faster than the one we were just on. And this will repeat until it's completely unsustainable on the next scale up. And it's all based on simple rules and it's predictable."

Unbounded Growth Requires Accelerating Cycles of Innovation to Avoid Collapse

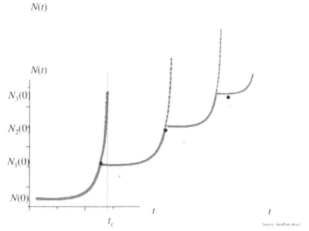

Hmm…. Where have we seen that before?

In Mr. West's work on cities, he states: "Once we started to urbanize, we put ourselves on this treadmill. We traded away stability for growth. And growth requires change."

Chapter 19

Terence McKenna

This is what I believe: That we are not pushed from behind by the casual unfolding of historical necessity, but that we are in the grip of an attractor of some sort, which lies ahead of us in time.-Terence McKenna.

T erence McKenna might not be a name familiar to the mainstream. However, he has a cult-like status among those who read his books and see his lectures.

McKenna created an idea about time called the Time-Wave Zero. It is based on fractal patterns he claimed to have discovered in the ancient divination text, the "I Ching." He proposed this predicted the end of time and a transition of consciousness in the year 2012. His promotion of this theory and its connection to the Maya calendar is credited as one factor leading to the widespread beliefs about 2012 eschatology.

I had never heard of him until after 2012 came and went.

Although he died in 2000, he still has a considerable presence on YouTube. Some of his audience - including his brother - had a troublesome time embracing his Time-Wave Zero idea. But I'm intrigued by the Time-Wave. And I want to defend it on his behalf.

What was his Time-wave Zero? From where I sit, it looks like the message of the market.

It is a notion where time has a structure and it follows a multifractal pattern. This pattern moves between periods of novelty and habit. Novelty complexifies and habit decays. In market-speak, boom and bust.

Events happening in a particular period resonate with other events happening in a different epoch. Each epoch is shorter than the one preceding it. As they get shorter and shorter, they will have a concrescence, omega point, or singularity. And this concrescence is approaching fast. McKenna came up with the theory in 1971 and put the omega point in December 2012.

Even though this idea was controversial, he was adamant this was the nature of time.

His critics seem to have gotten the last laugh, because he hooked his cart to December 21, 2012, for his zero point. As we all know, it didn't pan out. Yet, when I look at his Time-wave, it seems to suffer from only one grave error: choosing the date in 2012. He might have been too close to his work, but I suppose all he needed was an objective anchor date.

He chose 2012 because he was searching for a point of "maximum novelty." He looked at recent history for an event to anchor his Singularity date. He speculated the omega point must loom, and at most, it would be 500 years.

He settled on the atomic bomb in Hiroshima as his point of maximum novelty in recent history. Then it was a fractal of the Time-wave from there. This culminated in December 2012.

Later, McKenna discovered it serendipitously landed close to a major date in the Mayan culture; December 21, 2012. After hearing about it, this gave him a confirmation to stick to his date.

However, if he had lived longer, I'm confident McKenna would have abandoned this date well ahead of time. *"I will reexamine the dates if as we approached Dec 2012 progress wasn't accelerating at an unrecognizable pace.*" This wasn't happening yet. No A.I. robots were running around. We were still recognizable to ourselves.

The data points he used were large in scale. Thus, shifting his zero point to 2052 would keep all his time-wave comparisons valid. We can replace his Hiroshima conjecture with actual data points from the stock market. This reflects the collective barometer of economic novelty and habit. This removes the subjectivity.

Once again, the market was bigger than Terence. The market has voted. Building bombs is more novel than blowing them up.

I'll reiterate, we can't argue with the dates the stock market gives. They are the dates. We know the date of the Hiroshima bombing, but it is subjective to tie it to other historical points. If we built a database of all bombings and applied an LPPLS analysis to it, or a bifurcation map of it, one might get a quantifiable number. But I doubt it would calculate into Dec 2012.

The dates I laid out in Chapter 8 are quantifiable and have a mathematical relationship. The same mathematical relationship governing every complex process. The stock market data calibrates Terence's intuition with supporting non-subjective data. Unlike Terence, I didn't say these periods look like the 1960s, then analog those time periods. I did the opposite. The market said we mathematically relate to that time period, and lo and behold, the cultural climate also fractal.

2012 notwithstanding, Terence was a fantastic mind and orator. If you've never had the chance to hear him speak, check out some of his online videos and enjoy his unique eloquence.

If the predictions from the futurist in our next chapter play out, Terence - who had a wonderful sense of humor - could end up having the last laugh.

Chapter 20

Ray Kurzweil

Within a few decades, machine intelligence will surpass human intelligence, leading to The Singularity -- technological change so rapid and profound it represents a rupture in the fabric of human history. - Ray Kurzweil.

Ray Kurzweil has been talking about accelerating returns and its subsequent S curves of exponential gains for decades. He postulates after an S curve, another new exponential curve sets up. Then you have successive curves, one after another. He plots this for waves of technological advancement and talks about a "technological singularity", which he defines as computer power out-stripping human computational power.

Countdown to singularity

Singularity is technological change so rapid and so profound that is represents a rupture in the fabric of human history

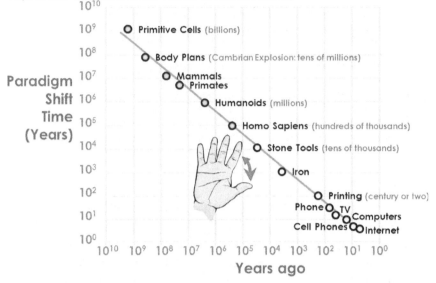

Some of his predictions have been bold and others slightly bizarre, but he has been spot on with his plotting of computational gains. I included him here because he has a simple message derived from looking at innovation and technology. It's a message of unstoppable speeding up growth happening at a scalable level.

Silicon Valley folklore weaves with Moore's law, like market isms to Wall Street. Kurzweil's predictions link with Moore's law, Metcalfe's law, and the less well-known Bell's law.

I'm not a fan of using these terms with the word law, because they aren't laws in the same way a power law, or the second law of thermodynamics, are laws. They are benchmarks for the growth of microprocessors (Moore's), network nodes (Metcalf), and computer systems (Bell's). They have followed the growth trends for these respected technologies for decades. If a law rests behind them, it could capture the Feigenbaum constants, or e and exponential growth, which would explain it.

As an interesting note, if we take Metcalf's law and apply it to Bitcoin's price, we back our way into capturing the fractal nature of how networks grow. When viewed through this lens, the movement in the price of Bitcoin becomes understandable. Its value has a direct relation to the number of nodes on the network. If the network grows, its value grows.

The De-Fi network will probably stay on its exponential curve, with nothing stopping it. But Bitcoin itself might lose its status within the network. Either way, the De-Fi of today traces out a path like the dot.com of 2000, only moving faster.

The Blockchain and its decentralized ledger will change the landscape and build the platform for the internet of things. Bitcoin will probably look like AOL, Yahoo, Netscape, or Amazon. Four different outcomes. The entire space will look like the internet of 2000 and change how we move information around.

But regardless, something Moore, Bell, Metcalf, and Kurzweil are all saying, is growth in technology more closely follows an exponential curve than a linear one.

Kurzweil's example goes: if you take 30 linear steps, you will have moved 30 steps. If you take 30 exponential steps, you will have moved 1 billion steps.

This is compounding on steroids.

Most exponential curves hit a wall and collapse. Skeptics have been calling for Moore's law to hit the wall for almost 50 years. And yet, the growth keeps coming.

These 30 steps equal a billion, has happened according to Kurzweil. He uses the smartphone as his example. He shows the smartphone has more processing power than the mainframe used by NASA to send the astronauts to the moon. And at a fraction of the cost. On a cost to performance basis, there has been a billion-fold increase.

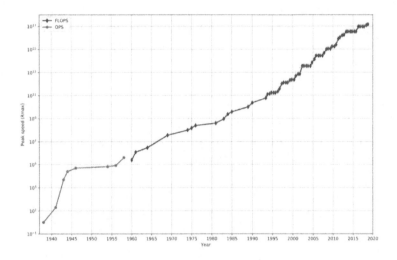

He claims if it keeps going for the next 30 years, humans won't recognize themselves by today's definition. Keep in mind, this chart has a log scale. Each progression arrives with a new zero at the end. To move up in scale requires a 10 fold move. It is mind-boggling if you stop to think about this transformation.

If he remains prescient about the growth not slowing down, he will probably remain correct about what it will imply. It's hard for our brains to wrap around this manner of growth. We linearly move through our day-to-day lives.

We understand the exponential growth of a baby in the womb. We notice the rapid growth from its minuscule size. But we also recognize the baby's growth slows down, or it would become a massive giant.

Geoffrey West refers to this type of growth as bounded growth. Human's experience bounded growth.

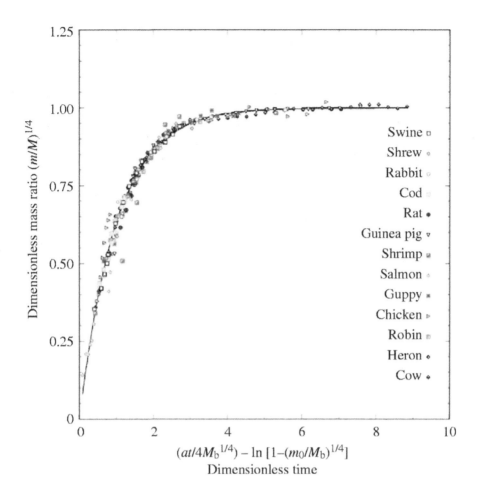

Dimensionless mass ratio $(m/M)^{1/4}$ versus $(at/4M_b^{1/4}) - \ln[1-(m_0/M_b)^{1/4}]$ Dimensionless time

Legend: Swine, Shrew, Rabbit, Cod, Rat, Guinea pig, Shrimp, Salmon, Guppy, Chicken, Robin, Heron, Cow

In their own image their world is fashioned
No wonder they don't understand - Neil Peart

In our defense, the future is not only faster than we think, it's faster than we *can* think. **The future will arrive fast and vast, and we move slow and small.**

His current call for technological singularity is 2045. Not too far from the 2052 capstone. Maybe he will be correct, and after 2045, the super-smart computers will do some amazing things for 7 years? Then who knows?

"An ecstatic view at an astonishing time."

Chapter 21

Benoit Mandelbrot

The techniques I developed for studying turbulence, like weather, also apply to the stock market. - Benoit Mandelbrot.

I assume most readers have heard of the Mandelbrot set. If you haven't, put down this book, go to the internet, and search for a video about it. Preferably one that zooms. Behold its image.

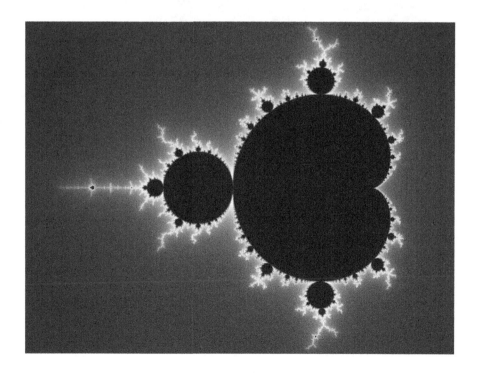

This set has slowly started to work it's way into our culture. The comedy show, performed by the Blue Man Group, had a skit about it. In the skit, they referred to it as "a real mind ****." Quite the understatement.

Sometimes when I look at multiple scales in index prices, the similarity feels like I'm in a real-life Mandelbrot zoom.

What is a zoom? It's when we keep going deep inside the set by going smaller and smaller. Check out this image from a magnification of 10^245!

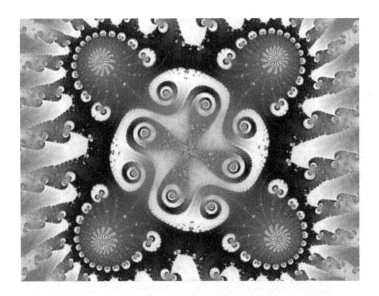

They made this image with math after going inside the set 245 orders of magnitude. To put it in perspective, that is many scales larger than our known universe.

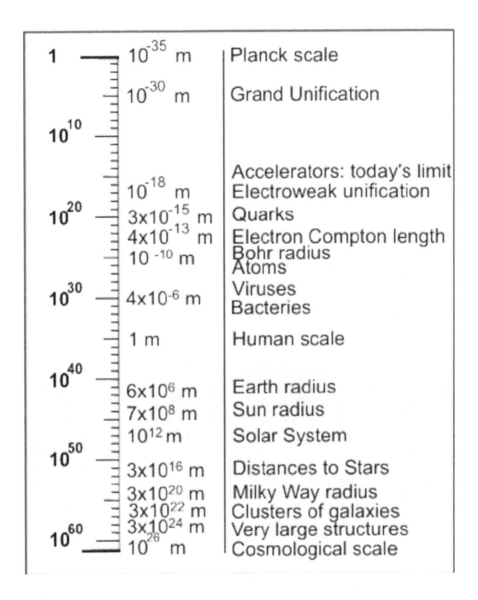

1	10^{-35} m	Planck scale
	10^{-30} m	Grand Unification
10^{10}		
	10^{-18} m	Accelerators: today's limit Electroweak unification
10^{20}	3×10^{-15} m	Quarks
	4×10^{-13} m	Electron Compton length
	10^{-10} m	Bohr radius Atoms
10^{30}	4×10^{-6} m	Viruses Bacteries
	1 m	Human scale
10^{40}	6×10^6 m	Earth radius
	7×10^8 m	Sun radius
	10^{12} m	Solar System
10^{50}	3×10^{16} m	Distances to Stars
	3×10^{20} m	Milky Way radius
	3×10^{22} m	Clusters of galaxies
10^{60}	3×10^{24} m	Very large structures
	10^{26} m	Cosmological scale

This complexity of the Mandelbrot set with all it's layers, emerges from this simple formula:

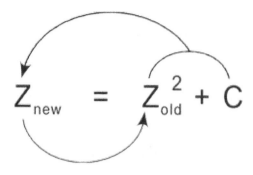

$$Z_{new} = Z_{old}^2 + C$$

It's astounding how at the core of this level of complexity lies this simplicity.

I'm including one more image. This image shows the relationship of the logistic map — from Chapter 12 — to the Mandelbrot set. It has been tilted to help visualize the fit.

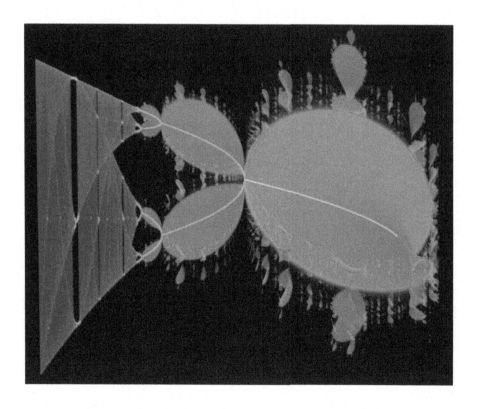

Benoit Mandelbrot created the set in 1980.

As a side note, Feigenbaum discovered his constants in 1975. In 1998, when Benoit wrote his famous book about fractals in finance, "The (Mis) Behavior of Markets," he never even mentioned Mitchell Feigenbaum or his constants. But we digress. Back to Mandelbrot and his set.

Mandelbrot changed how we make movies. He laid the foundation for how information moves in packets throughout the web. He mathematically answered how long a coastline is. Not to mention he created cool screensavers.

He worked on proofs of the markets being fractal and multifractal. He didn't believe in the Efficient Market Hypothesis. He showed how markets were like most things in nature and didn't follow a smooth curve.

He coined the word fractal. Surprising, because much of nature is fractal.

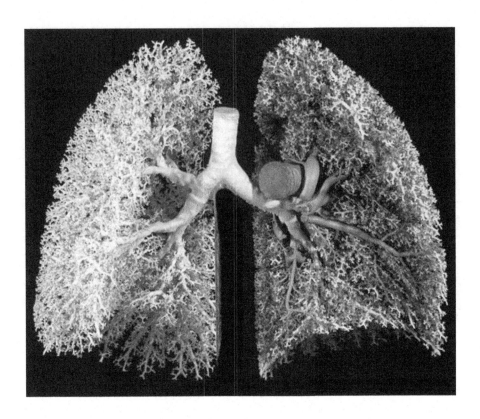

He passed away in 2010 but believed we have only scratched the surface of how to apply the science of fractals. He hoped others would take the ball and run down the court with it. Well, I hope this book plays its small part. What I would say to him was, "excellent pass."

Chapter 22

James Joyce

When I get to the bottom, I go back to the top of the slide
Where I stop, and I turn, and I go for a ride
'Til I get to the bottom, and I see you again!
Yeah, yeah, yeah! - "Helter Skelter." - John Lennon and Paul
McCartney.

Modern Library created a list of the 100 best novels of all time. James Joyce's "Ulysses" has the distinction of being the number one best fiction book ever written. I do not claim its merit. But, to win this distinction, people must resonate with something. (Fifty million Elvis Presley fans can't be all wrong)

Joyce lays out a pattern we somehow understand but is difficult to quantify. "The Tao that can be communicated isn't the Tao." - Lao Tzu.

Art is an attempt at communicating this impossibility. What we have here is verbal art. What is this artist trying to say?

The book is a lengthy and complex read. The entire plot contains one day in the life of a man living in Dublin. It's composed as an allegory and derives its name from the "Odyssey" by Homer.

The "Odyssey", accounts for the quest of Ulysses as he wanders his way home from battle. Along the way, he encounters many mythological tests.

This tying of one day with a decade-long quest provides a clue. Joyce challenges us to look at time as a fractal.

He uses a stream-of-consciousness writing, and through the character's musings, we follow a picture of a fractal universe. The writing isn't linear and exact. It's messy, fluid, and nonlinear.

He gave the reader an understanding of the entire picture of mankind, by recognizing the meaning and symbolism in one city block of Dublin. Joyce created a fractal narrative.

The idea of "as above so below" weaves a web of fractal time as well. Events from the past intertwine and link to both the present and the future. All human history is interacting with every other moment across various scales. It is a complex undertaking.

The book ends with a climactic 4391-word sentence. The word "yes" appears 27 times in this sentence. Enjoy the last 141 words from this sentence. Notice the spacing and rhythm of the word yes:

yes and all the queer little streets and pink and blue and yellow houses and the rosegardens and the jessamine and geraniums and cactuses and Gibraltar as a girl where I was a Flower of the mountain yes when I put the rose in my hair like the Andalusian girls used or shall I wear a red yes and how he kissed me under the Moorish wall and I thought well as well him as another and then I asked him with my eyes to ask again yes and then he asked me would I yes to say yes my mountain flower and first I put my arms around him yes and drew him down to me so he could feel my breasts all perfume yes and his heart was going like mad and yes I said yes I will Yes.- James Joyce.

The ending has a bubble crescendo. Building up and getting faster and faster into the final grandiose Yes.

The book mirrors the cycle of the market. The events appear to meander randomly. Then build a boom cycle with an ever-increasing frequency. Ending in a singularity. The yeses are like mini booms within the move. The spacing has a rhythm of speeding up at a steady pace of acceleration. I.e. the scaling of bifurcation points.

Also, the appearance of randomness before the boom takes hold is anything but. It is a wondrous tapestry and interrelated web. Many of the musings contain suffering, heartache, and pain, as setbacks happen along the way.

But like Homer's "Odyssey," the hero makes it home, and the end becomes an affirmation of Yes. The day and life become worth the suffering. Progress was a conclusion of the events.

In Joyce's sister's book to "Ulysses," "Finnegans Wake," the fundamental market pattern holds. We now move from the musings of one day with its climax ending, to the thoughts of the night and its bust.

The narrator has fallen asleep, and the stream becomes the subconscious. The crescendo of the boom has led to the bust. Joyce makes this clear by the following sentence from page one of Finnegan's Wake.

The fall (bababadalgharaghtakamminarronnkonnbronntonner-ronntuonnthunntrovarrhounawnskawntoohoohoordenenthur-nuk!)of a once wallstrait oldparr is retaled early in bed and later on life

The metaphor contains fractals. The fall happens on at least two scales, as it is "retaled early in bed" as we fall asleep and "later on life" as we die.

I built a graph of the spacing of these yeses, then coupled it with the fall from the first part of Finnegan's Wake. It's subjective. Maybe syllables would be a better match than words? Also, how far to make the crash was a subjective call. I chose 100% because there are 100 letters in the word representing the fall. I figured it was by design?

Chart 22-1

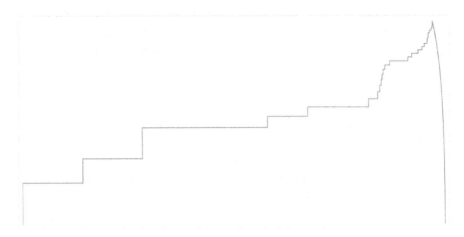

Now, Finnegan's Wake is also a circle. The first words are the last part of the last sentence of the book. Like the Mandelbrot set, the pattern is infinite. I included this passage in Chapter 11. I like it enough, I'll include it again:

The keys to. Given! A way a lone a last a love along the riverrun, past Eve and Adam's, from swerve of shore to bend of bay, brings us by a commodius vicus of recirculation — James Joyce.

"riverrun" - in small caps - is the first word of the book, and "the" - with no punctuation - is the last word of the book. It creates a circle. The book is without a beginning or an end.

Here lives one of history's greatest literary writers. He communicates a universal message the market also relays. A fractal world; interlinked, networked and intertwined. Repeating and rhyming, while moving, affirming, and building upon itself.

Part 3

Becoming the Butterfly.

It's the end of the world as we know it, and I feel fine. - R.E.M.

F rom the revelation chapter of the Bible to the modern sci-fi movies, there rests a tale of apocalypse or crisis type change in our western myths. We feel it; we sense it. Excitement and fear dance side by side within its song. Some behold a rapture, or peace after the battle. For others, it's enlightenment or peace after Samsara or suffering. For many, it holds a darker tone. Maybe a fierce fight with AI or an alien invasion.

The markets have something to say about these myths. Let's look.

Chapter 23

Sci Fi

I really wonder if we're creating our own successors with our constant desire for technological innovation and improvements. I wonder if this has been our destiny all along, and all of our pointless desires to possess the latest and greatest gadgets is just a program built into us that's fueling the creation of the next stage of life on earth. We are like insatiable caterpillars unaware that we are mindlessly building electronic cocoons which will give birth to gods.
- Joe Rogan.

Movies like The Terminator and The Matrix are popular franchises where AI has taken over. Elon Musk warns us that AI is a huge threat to humanity. *"Mark my words, AI is far more dangerous than nukes."* - Elon Musk.

Others are more optimistic. They envision robots doing the work humans don't want to do, freeing us to have better, more enjoyable lives. Some suggest we will merge to create a synergistic superhuman. But one thing the market states clearly; it is coming!

It seems imprudent to deny it or resist it.

If we went to early great apes and gave them the following choice. Stay great apes forever, or evolve into something unrecognizable to them. Something with bigger brains, more flexibility in movement, and the capacity to build flying machines. What would they choose?

Do we want to become something beyond who we are, or hold on to the familiar?

We don't have a say in this. Let's recall one of the first messages of the market; "go where it wants to go, not where you want it to go." The market divines "I am going forward. - I'm engineering novelty and complexity."

Our choice becomes getting on board or not.

Do the math. All species die. Some evolve past their previous selves, like Homo Erectus. Others, like the dodo bird, will never breathe again. Our only choice is to accept a new species of human will evolve, or prepare to be a dodo bird.

It's clear to me, 2052 will bring a capstone of a major scale. But how major? There are singularities at every scale. Singularities come in varieties beyond falling into a black hole.

When we fall asleep, the conscious day is over. Every day we are alive, we transform our awareness as we drift into sleep. This is a singularity.

Death also produces a singularity. One state of being transposed from another. I won't speculate here on what happens after we experience this singularity. Our form has shifted, while our DNA and our impact lives on.

The question becomes, what size scale of a bubble are we building culminating in 2052? Let's list some possibilities:

A) We will retrace a bubble the size of modern times. This began around 1440 AD after the printing press.

B) We will end the Holocene and retrace from 9700 BC.

C) We will retrace from the 300,000 years of Homo Sapiens.

D) We will become like the Dinosaurs sitting at 66 million years ago.

E) We will crescendo the entire process! I.e. all the way back to 13.57 billion years ago.

We have created a sci-fi scenario for each of these outcomes. The matching narrative for these scenarios goes something like this:

A) We will retrace a bubble the size of modern times. This began around 1440 AD after the printing press.

An American Indian chief goes for a ride across the country on a bus to discuss issues with the politicians. Along the way, he asked the driver if he could get off at the next stop to sit and wait for the next bus? The driver asked why. He replied, "so my soul can catch up". - Unattributed.

Under scenario A, no butterfly gets built yet. We merely have a MAJOR bear market. We digest the progress from the industrial revolution forward.

Crescendoing a 600-year bull market will require a large break to cascade into the next lower bowl. The down move would most likely be a 100-year bear market and a 50 to 80% loss of wealth gains. This loss will start from a much higher level than today.

This could play out in a couple of different ways.

Maybe we work on our humanity rather than our technology, so we don't burn or blow ourselves up. We step off the fast-moving hamster wheel and give ourselves time to catch up to the progress.

Or it could be a "Mad Max" sci-fi scenario. The "preppers" are betting on this outcome. Right or wrong looks like thirty years too soon.

B) We will end the Holocene and retrace from 9700 BC.

He seized the dragon, that ancient serpent, who is the devil, or Satan, and bound him for a thousand years. He threw him into the Abyss and locked and sealed it over him, to keep him from deceiving the nations anymore until the thousand years were ended. - Revelation 20:2-3

This manifests as the Anthropocene kicking into high gear. This creates a bear market from a 12,700 bull market crescendo. It would last 1000 to 2000 years and witness 50 to 80% of all life forms becoming extinct. Global warming or nuclear war could be the catalyst here.

It could be something geological. Nature has its rhythm of Feigenbaum bifurcation points. Think of asteroids, earthquakes, or volcano eruptions. They have a periodicity to them. And nature herself has defined the eons in a similar crescendo fashion without the help from the humans.

However, the Anthropocene playbook labels humans the responsible party. The thesis goes something like this: Humans are destroying their host planet. Our short-term thinking and hyper-growth will cascade out of control and lead to an extinction event some say has already started. Only they haven't agreed on the timing. Well, 2052 would give them the obvious reset they are looking for.

These 1000 years would also match up with some of the world's oldest and famous apocalyptic myths. Christianity, Judaism, and Zoroastrianism all have Millennial myths.

C) We will retrace from the 300,000 years of Homo Sapiens.

The ever-accelerating progress of technology and changes in the mode of human life gives the appearance of approaching some essential singularity in the history of the race beyond which human affairs, as we know them, could not continue. - John Von Neumann

300,000 years of Homo Sapiens could end via transcending into something of higher technology. Last time, our DNA carved out a cerebral cortex. This time, we might build our own silicon/techno brain. Thus, making current humans appear as intelligent as chimps. This is Ray Kurzweil's world. This is Joe Rogan's butterfly.

D) We will become like the Dinosaurs sitting at 66 million years ago.

Walking in your footsteps...
Hey mighty brontosaurus
Don't you have a lesson for us
You thought your rule would always last
There were no lessons in your past - Sting.

This would require some external shock or Anthropocene on steroids. No butterfly, because of no more humans. We become dodo birds and dinosaur bones.

The next 30 years could be our last climax. If so, enjoy it.

E) We will crescendo the entire process! I.e. all the way back to 13.57 billion years ago.

You are a divine being. You matter. You count. You come from realms of unimaginable power and light, and you will return to those realms... Love is what waits beyond. Love is being, in its purest sense. It is not becoming. It lies beyond the prison of culture, beyond the prison of ideology, beyond the prison of self-defined limitations. - Terence McKenna.

Scenario E is the butterfly on steroids. This is Homo Sapiens being part of a giant cosmic dance to wake up the multiverse. To end becoming and to be.

This is sci-fi beyond our current ability to imagine. This is Terence McKenna's world.

The message of the market foretells we have 30 years before we have to answer this multiple-choice test. So, this becomes fodder for a different time; a different book. So for now, let's go with the market and watch where the power law growth will take us.

We arrive in the present as the steward and witness to becoming butterflies. It seems pointless to hold on to the caterpillar.

We play our role in building this cocoon. Like the first mammals crawling out of the rubble after the catastrophic death of the dinosaurs. They created a new emergent life form which eventually gave us the homo sapiens. This is our ancestry, yet we have a better seat at the table.

Sure, it's depressing to see the next generation disconnected and narcissistically falling in love with their social media. But is it any different from how scary it was to the greatest generation when the counterculture of the 60s showed up with its sex, drugs, and rock n roll? In their way, the boomers figured things out. Now this new generation, with its way of disconnecting by digitally connecting, will also figure it out.

The sixties could visualize the liberation of the butterfly, however, we needed to build the cocoon. Now, we can comprehend the techno prison of the Chrysalis under construction. No more caterpillar, but what a grand notion being part of a superstructure metamorphosis for humanity.

Chapter 24

We are Cells in the Network

Still she haunts me, phantomwise,
Alice moving under skies
Never seen by waking eyes.

Children yet, the tale to hear,
Eager eye and willing ear,
Lovingly shall nestle near.

In a Wonderland they lie,
Dreaming as the days go by,
Dreaming as the summers die:

Ever drifting down the stream —
Lingering in the golden gleam —
Life, what is it but a dream? - A Boat Beneath a Sunny Sky , Lewis
Carroll.

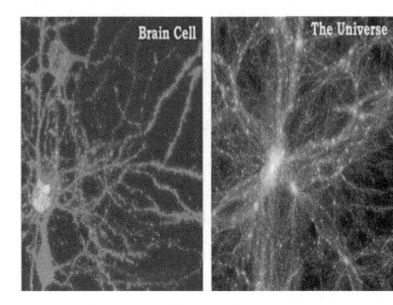

The universe looks like a giant brain. *"If it's the brain, where's the body?"*–Aine, age 12, Edinburgh, UK

This was a question posed by "Curious Kids.'' Where kids write in and ask scientists questions. This shortened answer given for this question was there is no body. They simply look alike, because rules govern the universe, and one of those rules is fractals.

But sometimes, the kids see things clearer than the scientist.

Let's stay with this metaphor for a minute rather than be dismissive. What if the universe is multifractal, not merely fractal? Does this imply a body?

A discovery of this body could solve the theory of everything problem plaguing physics. And by body, I don't mean a human body. Rather, something larger than our known universe, in which our universe is a subset. I.e. The body is the next bowl up.

When theoretical physics talks of a multiverse, and parallel universes, and superstrings, or cycles of time, aren't they talking about "the body?"

Indra, the ancient Hindu God, has an infinite net. This net has a multifaceted jewel in every vertex. These jewels reflect all the other jewels.

Hindus also have Vishnu, who dreams the universe into existence and holds it in a lotus flower in the palm of his hand. He echoes a metaphor for the body.

Buddha states: *"the fields full of assemblies, the beings, and eons which are as many as all the dust particles, are all present in every particle of dust."*

In Lewis Carroll's famous book, "Through the Looking Glass," Alice is told she is within the dream of the Red King. And if he awakes, she will go out *"like a light."* The quote at the beginning of this chapter, lies at the end of Lewis Carroll's book, and it adds another layer of complexity. Because Alice herself is but a dream. Therefore, the Red King becomes multifractal.

These myths touch a significant part of our cultures for a reason. Carl Jung, the swiss psychiatrist, referred to this as our collective unconscious. It is shared by all, intuited by all, yet elusive to all. The 12-year-old girl sees it clearer than the scientist.

I find it amazing we have the technology to create the photo. Humans have mapped the galaxy clusters, and the network of neurons in our brain. What an accomplishment on both ends.

Because we built the technology creating this photo, we live with the implications. And the implications are profound. It's superfluous if the scientist stands correct in the direct correlation. The 12-year-old notices the obvious. It's now the scientist's job to go figure it out.

To become the fish understanding it's swimming in water. This photo operates like the fish tasting the air beyond the water.

Earlier, we spoke of the leaf, branches and trees being self similar. Geoffrey West shows us how the forest is a fractal as well.

Relation between number and diameter of trees in a forest recapitulates the branches of the largest trees

$$N \propto D^{-2} \propto M^{-3/4}$$

The multifractal nature of the stock market implies more scales as well. The current view of dark energy isn't sufficient. A message of the market; keep foraging.

Maybe the Galaxy clusters behave like the brain of The Red King, or Yahweh, or Shiva. Maybe the milky way rests like a cell in this brain. And our solar system functions like an atom in the brain cell. And Earth rotates like an electron of the atom. And life on earth bounces like quarks on the atom. And our atoms on earth mirror the Planck scale to our atoms.

The matching here is hypothetical. It's not meant as an accurate representation. Rather, a metaphor. A multifractal way of viewing our place in the multiverse.

Allow me to illustrate with an example scenario:

This is a chart of the known Electromagnetic spectrum.

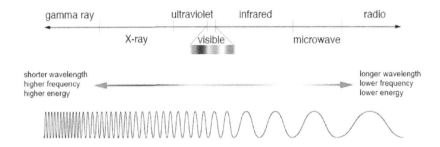

Notice how little of the spectrum we see as humans. It took some fantastic science to look beyond. Then find, prove, and use the scale beyond what we see.

Is the universe vaster than we can currently see, prove and use? Most likely.

This is a musing after listening to the market.

Chapter 25

Pushing the Edge.

So put me on a highway
And show me a sign
And take it to the limit one more time. - "Take it to the Limit." -
Glenn Lewis Frey / Don Henley / Randy Meisner.

Trey Parker and Matt Stone created the animated comedy series "South Park." It has run for over 24 years. They have produced 9 films, 4 soundtracks, and an awesome Broadway show. They are prolific, popular, and creative comedians. They also push the edge.

Sometimes when we push the edge, we go too far. These guys have done things so clever, creative, and hilarious, I'm envious of their genius. Occasionally, I watch something they have done and say, that didn't work; it was over the line. This ability to press it is part of their genius.

In this book, I will state something that goes awry. I would rather go too far and get the conversation going than leave something out. I trust it won't tarnish the intent of the book.

I say this because this chapter is speculative. I don't have a degree in theoretical physics and I'm not smart enough to get one. I know enough about the topic to get myself in trouble.

"Knowing what you don't know is more important than being brilliant." - Charlie Munger

No one knows where 4.6692 comes from, or the source of its universality. I'll throw out this speculation at the risk of harming the credibility of the presentation of the forecast.

All protons have ½ spin and an identical mass of $1.6726 * 10^{-24}$

The market has ½ spin and bifurcates at a ratio of the cube root of 4.6692 which is 1.6714.

The Planck scale is currently the smallest known measurement in our universe. A current estimate of the number of planks fitting inside a proton $1.6714 * 10^{-24}$.

Hmm, curiouser and curiouser.

Is this a coincidence or a clue? A plausible conclusion would be a holographic multiverse. It would explain the multifractals. It could tie in where the Feigenbaum constant is coming from. It could also remove the quandary between general relativity and quantum mechanics.

I'm not saying this is so. I'm trying to understand the implications of an attractor in the future. How does this fit with our limited world view? Answering these questions contains part of the purpose of writing this book.

It's currently beyond my education and understanding. I would enjoy discussing it. Feedback is awesome. If you can assist, call me.

If this goes somewhere, fantastic. If it falls flat, at least I kept the chapter short.

Part 4

Everyday Applications.

That's the way that the world goes round, your up one day, the next your down. It's a half an inch of water and you think you're going to drown. That's the way that the world goes round. - John Prine.

The primary purpose of the book centers on aligning oneself with the markets to realize financial profits. But I hope the message spreads wider. Living a fully balanced life would have us all healthy, wealthy, wise, related, and enjoying the show.

Therefore, this part of the book contains practical applications of the message of the stock market.

Chapter 26

Self

It's the circle of life
And it moves us all
Through despair and hope
Through faith and love
'Til we find our place
On the path unwinding
In the circle
The circle of life - Elton John and Tim Rice.

This chapter is proving problematic for me. Ironic wouldn't you say. Maybe because we "teach best what we need to learn most." I'm not a writer to begin with, and I apologize for this transparency in my presentation. But, I have stumbled, more than usual, every time I sit down to compose this chapter.

Part 4 of the book has scales in mind with its structure. Self contains the starting point of further levels. Yet, it feels arrogant to claim enough understanding of one's self, to impart ideas of self to the other. I hardly have the wisdom to navigate myself.

I must be an acrobat
To talk like this
And act like that - Acrobat - Bono

But what I can say, with resolute clarity, is: be humble in our successes and empathetic with our failures. If we're alive, we will experience both. And so too will our family, friends, and foes.

How is this a message of the market? Well, because everything rises and falls. Ebb and flow. We can't stop it.

You can pause the market, but it will re-open with a vengeance.

The markets illustrate a constant interplay between boom and bust. Fear and greed. Success and failure. It's not possible to have one without the other. It hasn't changed since we have been measuring it.

Black and white, dance side by side; each part containing the other. And within each part lies a Yin and Yang to itself. Multiple levels cascade and interweave endlessly. Along the boundary, between the two, contains the edge where they surf both sides. Separate yet united.

The markets do this on many scales. Scales beyond my ability to grasp. Beyond anyone's ability to grasp. A massive Mandelbrot diagram of mathematically related boom and busts inside a miraculous dance.

Our choice becomes how we want to take part in its unfolding. To discover how we can best surf this edge of chaos.

Bob Dylan sang, *"Beauty walks a razor's edge, someday I'll make it mine."*

We mirror yin yang symbols placed within a web of larger and smaller symbols. Dancing and crashing. Loving and falling. Living and dying. Celebrating the opportunity of participating in the process. And experience the pain and sorrow accompanying it.

As Joseph Campbell put it, *"To joyously participate in the sorrows of life."*

Empathy stands as the white dot inside the darkness of failure. Humble sits as the black dot inside the light of success.

I went to the quotation well frequently in this chapter. I needed the help of outside wisdom more than usual. And with that, I'll call on one more piece of wisdom to close this chapter.

Father forgive us for what we must do.
You forgive us, we'll forgive you.
We'll forgive each other til we both turn blue,
then we'll whistle and go fishin in heaven.- John Prine.

Chapter 27

Family

The other night I ate at a real nice family restaurant. Every table had an argument going. — George Carlin.

What do CAS, Feigenbaum, and stock prices have to do with the family? Well...

Families function as our own private complex adaptive systems. They hold our direct DNA and our epigenetic codes. They also contain feedback loops. Therefore, if CAS can help with predicting weather and stocks, there should be applications for the family as well.

The purpose of this book is larger than money, or I wouldn't have even gone to the trouble of writing it.

As soon as I let this idea out into the public domain, I have killed any edge from remaining proprietary. It's out there. I have shared it. - Or more accurately, sold it for the price of a book. Hardly an effective get-rich-quick plan.

Types of Headaches

Migraine

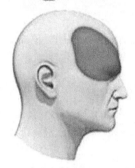

Hypertension

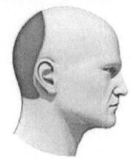

Stress

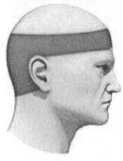

Writing a book

@WritersResource

IF my theory is valid, and I've communicated it well enough, and I get lucky and it reaches an audience, THEN swarms of machine learning programs will go to work and start incorporating this model and producing improvements. Thus rendering my hand-produced outcomes sophomoric. Therefore, my greatest value is putting the ideas out there and letting the programs go to work. And hopefully help you, the reader, incorporate this frame into your thinking.

A fun place becomes foraging for fractals in our family.

Let's start with DNA. We share direct DNA with our biological family. When the egg and the sperm from our parents fused, it began the process of creating us. At that moment, there were many factors already predictable about us. They created our genome; it was fixed, and it was going to operate its program. How tall we were, our eye color, our hair color, the shape of our face, were already set, and it was going to happen.

Diet and nurturing will have some effect on these physical traits, but only at the margin.

Where we will be on a random January day, and what we will wear, remains unknown. But we can identify our size, motor skills, and appearance. Geoffrey West postulates that we might even have a fixed number of heart beats encoded in our software.

If something on a larger scale disrupts this DNA process, the prediction will fall apart. Say if we get hit by a bus, or lose a finger in an accident. But barring that, the instruction code demands our process proceed.

Where we live, our level of education, and how many resources we have available to us, have predictable pathways. Networks have patterns in how they behave. We can create excellent probability trees to recognize when and how people move around. Once again, this type of prediction will have a fuzzy or 'strange' map to it. But we can make patterns and generalizations.

What trust do we have with our family? We can predict each other's behavior. We trust the sun will rise because it's reliable. We aren't as predictable as the sun, thus we aren't as trustworthy. We are irregular and messy, but only to a point. That's how our families 'know' us.

I contend it's deeper. I realize I'm traveling down a slippery slope, but if we can show something is going on here, and quantify it, the slope won't be so slippery anymore. We accomplish this with data analysis. And now we have significant amounts of data.

Even before actively collecting the data, we perform this with our families all the time. We talk about how someone is stuck in a rut or makes the same mistakes. But we also notice progress and aha moments. We learn from our mistakes as we concurrently keep repeating them.

What I assert is, if we apply the framework of the message of the market to data within our families, we will see patterns and be able to quantify these aspects as well.

I've already mentioned Facebook, Google, and Amazon collecting this information about us and our families. These patterns, within the data, will shape their way into how we understand ourselves.

If you hunt for these self-similar situations in aspects of your own family life, it could lead to a simple change in expectations. I'm not implying a lowering of your expectations, rather a re-framing of them.

If a bear market lurks on the horizon, it would be foolish to force the market to stay up; the only way to profit is to "go with the flow."

The same holds for our loved ones. It's foolish to expect every day to arrive as an up day. When we prepare for a bear market, it becomes less taxing when it arrives. Why would our loved ones only be cheerful and always in bull markets? Also, with time, the troublesome periods become less and less deep. They get resolved quicker. We construct progress.

Now, let's examine feedback. Feedback is necessary to any dynamic system. Without feedback, the system dies.

Family and friends provide our number one source of feedback. Maybe we resist, thus giving in to a flawed strategy. We die without feedback. Luckily, our families and friends keep us alive by giving us more love than we care to take in.

So, be sure to thank those in your life as they nudge you along your growth curves. They keep things vibrant and robust.

Chapter 28

Career

Plus ça change, plus c'est la même chose

The more that things change, the more they stay the same. -Jean-Baptiste Alphonse Karr.

As little as three generations ago, over 80% of humans were farmers. Now it's less than 5%. So over 75% of previous workers lost their jobs. Technology displaced all of them. Disruption is nature's way, and now it's happening fast.

How can we apply this in our investments or career? Let's start by looking at a significant sector of the economy; the retail sector.

In 1974, Sears and Roebuck moved into the tallest building in the world; the Sears Tower. They held the title of the world's largest retailer. Their catalogs disrupted the industry and put many other retailers out of business. The stock hit an all-time high after a 40-year bull run. They belonged to a group of stocks collectively known as the nifty fifty growth stocks.

At this same time, a new retailer had gone public; Sam Walton's Walmart. When the growth stock bubble burst, most of the nifty fifty companies' stock prices fell by 50 to 80%; Sears tumbled 73% and Walmart dropped 83%. After the dust settled, and the subsequent up wave started, the baton had passed to Walmart.

Fast forward to 2000, and Walmart had put many mom-and-pop retailers out of business and put a huge dent in Sears supremacy. The

Walton family was the wealthiest family on the planet, as Walmart stock was putting the final touches on a 25-year bull run.

Peter Lynch managed the legendary Magellan fund for Fidelity Investments. He coined the term 10-bagger to describe a company whose stock prices went up 10 fold. He spoke of the rare 100-bagger. A stock gaining 100 times your investment.

From its low in 1975 to its high in 2000, Walmart was a 7000-bagger. You read that right; a well-timed one thousand dollar investment became worth 7 million dollars. Meanwhile, Sears sat in its twenty-five-year reign in the world's tallest headquarters, with a stock moving nowhere.

At the top in 2000, another less well-known retailer had recently gone public;. Amazon.

In the subsequent dot.com bust, Amazon's stock plummeted 95%. But the seeds are also sewn. When the dust settled, the baton had passed again. Fast forward to today, and now Jeff Bezos is the richest person on the planet, as Amazon created new businesses while destroying others. They again changed how the world shopped.

After the frightening 95% plunge, from its low in 2001, until its recent high in 2021, Amazon gave investors a 600-bagger. Walmart's stock went nowhere for over 15 years. And Sear's lost all its glory, and its name-sake tower now stands as the Willis Tower.

Now, a new company has gone public with its stock. Over the next two years, its price will fall as today's growth stocks fall out of favor. And fifteen years from now, retail will have shifted again. And a huge bagger lies in wait.

Sears disrupted retail with the catalog; speeding up how we shopped. Walmart optimized the supply chain and changed the way we shopped. Amazon brought items from our digital devices straight to our front door.

What could come faster than free overnight or even 2-hour delivery? Well, how about 3D printers? We will build what we need right in our own homes. No need to travel to the store or have items shipped.

So here sits a suggestion. If retail is your career or your investment forte, do a bit of research, and find a company bringing delivery straight into the home. If you're an investor, buy the stock. If you're a worker, go to work for the company, keep all your stock options, and fifteen years from now, you will look like a clairvoyant. But get ready, because as the market goes parabolic again, a new giant will emerge.

Retail isn't your thing, then how about consumer technology? The waves are analogous with similar dates. Instead of Sears, it was the television. Instead of Walmart, it was the computer. Instead of Amazon, it was the smartphone.

What's next in consumer tech? Likely it's wearable's. The TV brought news and entertainment to the home. Computers brought faster and personalized news and entertainment to the home. The smartphone puts personalized news and entertainment in the palm of our hands.

A whole new industry with fantastic job opportunities and huge wealth creation will unfold for the companies bringing the technology onto our bodies or even inside our bodies. Do a bit of research, then buy those stocks or work with one of those companies. You will have job security and wealth creation while others around you will get laid off and look for new work/careers.

You can use this template for multiple industries and careers. You can now gauge how long the cycle will last. This will help not only with the financial aspects but hopefully reduces the anxiety of the uncertainty we face.

If a key to happiness resides in proper expectations, then this re-frame will help create happiness. The uncertainty will shift towards opportunity. We can ditch the anxiety and become aligned with the fresh growth and wealth transformation ahead of us.

The days of working the same job during our lifetime are over for most industries. However, we also have the opportunity to create the same amount of wealth in a shorter amount of time.

It took Sears eighty years to reach its pinnacle. For Walmart, the time dropped to fifty years. Amazon accomplished its amazing feat in twenty-seven years. Future dynasties will rise from scratch in a mere fifteen years. We won't need to be the CEO to take part in the fast and vast new wealth creation opportunities. We can accomplish a lifetime in less than two decades.

The red line on the cover of this book travels the same distance as the green line. The red line represents ten years of Tesla's stock price. The green line chronicles seven centuries of wheat. Kings and Queens held their rule of taxing and controlling the food production of our farms. This control lasted centuries because innovation remained slow. Today, relative kings and queens will spontaneously emerge and accomplish in decades what took our ancestors centuries.

The blockchain already creates new wealth even faster than Tesla did. The 'internet of things' will change our world. Any technology or company sitting front and center, will create massive wealth in short order.

As compounding periods speed up and become relative, getting rich quickly will become a reality, not a pipe dream. Looking at annual returns will soon become superfluous.

In my career, it's easy to see the time frame speeding up. Only a few sophisticated players once used options. Initially, the expiration cycle was quarterly. Then came the monthly option. Now, weekly options prevail, and the options market has become larger than the stock market. The tail is wagging the dog!

Soon the daily option will become the norm.

As the cycle speeds up, so too must the compounding interval. So fear not if you are behind on your retirement plan. The market will provide the opportunity to catch up.

It's stressful to learn a new career, but it can also be enjoyable learning something new. To create novelty; to grow. Looks like we will get plenty of opportunities.

Chapter 29

Society

I can tell you fancy, I can tell you plain. You give something up for everything you gain. Since every pleasure's got an edge of pain, pay for your ticket and don't complain. - "Silvio." - Bob Dylan.

S teven Pinker has done some admirable work on how by almost any measure life is becoming "better." He created an excellent Ted talk illustrating this. It's a significant find for anyone who likes to look at the big picture.

In his book "Enlightenment Now," he breaks down 15 measures of well-being like literacy, life span, crime rates, etc, and shows how they all have improved. And yet, our perception says otherwise?

If life is getting better, then how come it doesn't feel like it?

The boom-bust cycle of life creates challenges to begin with. Now compound this with the speeding up rate of change.

We seem to wish things smooth and stable, but that's not how nature works. Fat tails rule and fat tails bring with them change. Smooth and stable causes death. Boom and bust create life.

Allow me to use a metaphor of the water or river's edge. The party and the battle happen here. Here lies the edge of chaos.

As we move more and more towards the shore, features become less dynamic, more ensconced. In a word, more stable. By the time we reach the mountain top, change becomes trivial and life becomes negligible. Above the treeline, things get stable fast. Life exists up here, but it's a far less complex and dynamic environment.

Conversely, as we move in the opposite direction, out deeper and deeper into the water, things become more chaotic. It's no longer the edge of chaos, it has become chaos. Life exists out in the deep water of the oceans, but it's also far less complex and dynamic.

For humans, and most life forms, the message is simple: move too far inland or towards stability and you will probably die. Move too far out to sea, or towards chaos, and you will probably drown.

The edge is where it's at. It's also messy and full of risks and rewards. Our most expensive real estate sits at the water's edge; be it a lake, a river, or the ocean. While it's the most valuable, it's also where the fat tails hang out.

Life can be challenging at the edge. We incorrectly wish for an easy and stable environment. We deplore fat tails. Maybe this explains why we call bubbles manias? They carry such a negative connotation. And after bubbles pop, some people get hurt.

The NASDAQ bubble, ending in 2000, hurt anyone who only played the market at the top. But fortunes were created, and the internet got built. Everyone now has history, maps, education, data, and cat pictures in the palm of their hand.

Without the mania, it never would have happened. There wasn't some magic formula where the Federal Reserve and the politicians could have created the growth in some smooth fashion, keeping everything nice and orderly. Manias are part of the process.

I would postulate anyone buying Tesla at the start of 2021 will probably lose money. It is by any definition a bubble or mania. And pain, greed, and envy rule on Wall Street. But pain, greed, and envy will push the ball of progress down the court.

The fantastic profits made by people who got in early on Tesla will lead others to follow; i.e. act manic. They want to "get in on it." So money, talent, and the focus move towards building cleaner cars, better energy storage, efficient production, and automation.

What will this bring? Safer cars, faster production, better use of energy, and a reallocation of resources. Today's Tesla stockholder will be a victim of its success. After the stock falls - which it will - pundits will march out with the mania and bubble talk. They will talk about the money "lost."

Anyone who bought Cisco at the top of the internet bubble isn't a happy camper. It didn't work out for anyone buying the high. But the company produced tremendous amounts of money and provided the backbone to the network we surf on every day all over the planet.

The company has generated over $130 billion in profits. The tangible type. The ones we can spend. It possesses a current market capitalization of $200 billion. It has made many people rich and created a value-added product for our digital network.

Yet, those who bought the high in 2000 have lost half of their money and missed out on 20 years of large gains in other assets.

Few participants bought only the top. And likely some of the biggest losers were the index funds forced to buy it as its market cap grew. This happened to Tesla recently when it became part of the S&P500 index. The money buying the stock as it came into the S&P500, will probably be underwater 10 years from now, while the market itself will be much higher.

The risk becomes spread throughout the system, and thus Tesla is playing its part in moving us forward. Well done.

The smart money will sell and move on. The hype has everyone wanting in and the competition will become fierce. Tesla has become the shark too big for the territory. It's so prominent even the small piranhas are circling. They want in on all the food Tesla is receiving.

So they will start ferociously eating from below the food chain. And 10 years from now there will be some piranha coming out of the Tesla frenzy and creating massive gains for anyone working there or buying its stock. They will be like the new Amazon coming out of the internet bubble.

As the piranha's circle from below, the killer whales circle from above. Existing auto manufacturers are envious of Tesla, and they will fight to get in on the frenzy they missed out on. They have immense resources, and they will funnel them in the new direction of self-driving cars and cleaner energy. And they will do it like a pack of killer whales coming for the shark.

The water holds another threat; shark hunters. These include Google, UBER, and LYFT. Apple also says they want in. And Amazon and Facebook most likely won't sit by and let someone else control the roads. GE is far smaller now than Tesla, but still retains enormous resources, and they have admitted they are envious of Tesla's battery factories. And envy is powerful.

Witness a complex system in action. Tesla had a fat tail moment to the upside. Now it will have its fat tail to the downside. We will see if it acts like AOL, and go buy a company like General Electric. Or it might go the way of Cisco, and build huge profits but have all the profitability built into its price. Or it could go the way of YAHOO and slowly bleed out. But it will fall from these exponential gains. (Time of writing Feb 2021).

Should Congress or the exchanges have stepped in and stopped its exponential rise, so the immature johnny-come-lately doesn't get hurt? Should the pundits scream from high heaven to stop the mania?

Or, how about we celebrate the fat tail and realize without it, the piranhas and the killer whales and shark hunters may never have shown up? It's all part of the process. The only way to stop it is to kill it.

The message of the market is to embrace the bubble and accept its behavior. Find out what part you want to play in its unfolding. Because it's going to happen. If Elon Musk wouldn't have led the charge, someone else would have. Hat's off to Elon, he has the entire world watching.

Chapter 30

Humanity

Meanwhile back in the year one
When you belonged to no one
You didn't stand a chance, son
If your pants were undone
'Cause you were bred, for humanity
And sold to society
One day you'll wake up, in the present day
A million generations removed from expectations
Of being who you really want to be
Skating away, skating away, skating away
On the thin ice of the new day - "Stating Away." - Ian Anderson.

A s a species, humanity wakes up in 2021 in the throes of the late stages of a grand crescendo; at the capstone of a huge pyramid of evolution.

Humans behave in a brutal, dirty, and destructive manner to our home planet. Yet we hold beauty, industriousness, and the sublime. Yin and Yang.

It's an improbable coincidence humankind shows up in a direct Feigenbaum relationship to evolution. And the industrial revolution shows up with a direct Feigenbaum relationship to ourselves. And the industrial revolution has a direct Feigenbaum relationship to the smartphone I'm using right now.

This hidden order escapes conjecture; it's grounded in math and science. And we have a prominent seat at the table.

As a species, we only have one opportunity to burn the fossil fuels we consume. They took millions of years to build, as we consume them in far less than a millennium.

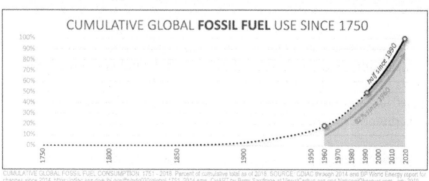

CUMULATIVE GLOBAL **FOSSIL FUEL** USE SINCE 1750

CUMULATIVE GLOBAL FOSSIL FUEL CONSUMPTION 1751 - 2018. Percent of cumulative total as of 2018. SOURCE: CDIAC through 2014 and BP World Energy report for changes since 2014. https://cdiac.ess-dive.lbl.gov/ftp/ndp030/global.1751_2014.ems. CHART by Barry Saxifrage at VisualCarbon.org and NationalObserver.com. July 2019.

But we have an enormous capacity to innovate, and we have millions of people working on the problem of dirty and limited fossil fuels.

We ride on the edge of chaos, but it appears we will surf the edge and resolve the crisis facing humanity. We have the computer power, the human resources, and the willpower to do it. We, humans, claim proclivity at making messes, yet proficiency in cleaning them up.

In his career as a physicist, Fritjof Capra came to the following conclusion: Quantum theory thus reveals a basic oneness of the universe. It shows that we cannot decompose the world into independently existing smallest units. As we penetrate into matter, nature does not show us any isolated "building blocks," but rather appears as a complicated web of relations between the various parts of the whole. These relations always include the observer in an essential way. The human observer constitutes the final link in the chain of observational processes, and the properties of any atomic object can be understood only in terms of the object's interaction with the observer.

The market tells the same message. We feel controlled by the pull of the attractor, but we sense we interact by pushing it there. We built the stock exchanges and public companies trading on them. Yet, the pull beckoned us from its place. We take part in the feedback system, but the system contains vastness beyond any isolated player.

Trading on the floor in the exchanges back in the 90s encapsulated a metaphor of the entire process. Traders were competing for the best orders while cooperating to maintain all the flows moving. The traders had to cooperate or the whole thing would fall apart. Yet, they had to compete to hold the system robust and to gain their advantage.

The entire exchange also bifurcated many times. It moved from a room full of chalkboards to a pit full of clerks and runners moving the orders. Then toward people wearing headsets wired with sophisticated communication lines. Then shifting to a web of computers with a human pointing and clicking the order flows with a mouse and a keyboard. To the computers running the show.

Humanity mirrors this process. The web of humanity bifurcates through our stages of progress. We moved from the egg of our ancient ancestors to become a caterpillar. We are now creating the Chrysalis, a lengthy process where we are now at the capstone. Then onward towards the butterfly, with powers and freedom beyond our grasp.

It requires all of us to compete and cooperate. To follow the path laid out before us while simultaneously pressing the progress. To surf the duality and embrace the oneness. To build the bomb, but never blow it up.

This is our role in the process of humanity. The stakes feel high because the system is wondrous.

Our ancestors worked agonizingly and endured far worse than us. And they did this work without modern pain medication. They suffered through famines, plagues, volcanoes, hurricanes, wildfires, and earthquakes. All without FEMA., the Red Cross, and clean water. But they survived. We owe it to them to keep weaving the web of complexification. The market demands we press on; we have a place in the fabric of time.

Chapter 31

God

All religions, arts and sciences are branches of the same tree. -
Albert Einstein.

Why bring up God in a book about markets and Feigenbaum constants. Well, because...

Humans are a religious species. Our spiritual nature separates us from other animals. We have an added level of complexity.

There are 5 dominant religions, 12 primary religions, with about 4,300 total. Yet, within these categories, there are further branches. We have an estimated 41,000 different Christian religions alone. Think about that.

We long for a connection to something higher than ourselves. We intuitively recognize it's there, but it eludes us. "What you don't know you can feel somehow". - Beautiful Day - Bono.

We keep circling back towards the intrinsic nature.

We have a sense of belonging. A sense of purpose. Being part of something larger than ourselves. When this meaning becomes dogmatic or empty, we press forward or circle back to get at the Tao, or the source, or nature, or Yahweh, or...

These are traits of being with complexity; us recognizing who we are. Some suggest it's emergent. Some claim it's inherent. But we perceive it's there.

What is the level of consciousness of a Redwood tree monitoring countless seasons come and go? It's been a part of fires and infestations, as it majestically stands above all else in the forest. What does it experience? What is its larger fractal extending beyond the forest?

Mankind ponders these topics and works towards understanding them.

What drives this passion for growth and understanding? Are we being pushed from our genes and ancestors, or are we being guided or pulled by some strange force?

What about the immigrant worker who gave his life building the last part of the Transcontinental Railroad in the middle of the barren Nevada, Utah desert? He played his part creating the network, enabling the flow of people, goods, and information across the continent. One elemental cell in the foundation of our infrastructure. Operating like blood cell in our body's, giving their short life, so we can be conscious.

We, humans, function like blood cells in the unseen body.

And we, as a planet, are like pinealocytes in the pineal gland of the Red King from "Through the Looking Glass." We are doing our part to spark the imagination inside his dream, as he sends us signals on how to proceed.

Such is the world of multifractals. It's far more compelling than a meaningless big bang somehow springing out of nowhere. Terence McKenna had this to say about a meaningless big bang:

"We are asked by science to believe that the entire universe sprang from nothingness, at a single point, and for no discernible reason. This notion is the limit case for credulity. In other words, if you can believe this, you can believe anything. It is a notion that is, in fact, utterly absurd, yet terribly important. Those so-called rational assumptions flow from this initial impossible situation. Western religion has its own singularity in the form of the apocalypse, an event placed not at the beginning of the universe but at its end. This seems a more logical position than that of science. If singularities exist at all, it seems easier to suppose that they might arise out of an ancient and highly complexified cosmos, such as our own, than out of a featureless and dimensionless mega-void."

Nietzsche and Darwin declared God dead, but the markets bring god back into life and into focus.

How did the markets give us back this notion of something beyond ourselves? Because they operate as though they realize where they are going. They have a purpose. They have a plan. They have a memory and intelligence. Currently, we can only speculate on the source. But we can grasp it and measure it.

James Joyce witnessed it. Einstein visualized it. Lao Tzu coded it. Terence McKenna perceived it. Thoreau felt it in simplicity. Jason Silva grabs it in complexity.

Stuart Kauffman, a biologist studying complexity for decades, titled his book about the subject, "At Home in the Universe." Here is a quote from the book.

"If biologists have ignored self-organization, it is not because self-ordering is not pervasive and profound. It is because we biologists have yet to understand how to think about systems governed simultaneously by two sources of order. Yet who seeing the snowflake, who seeing simple lipid molecules cast adrift in water forming themselves into cell-like hollow lipid vesicles, who seeing the potential for the crystallization of life in swarms of reacting molecules, who seeing the stunning order for free in networks linking tens upon tens of thousands of variables, can fail to entertain a central thought: if ever we are to attain a final theory in biology, we will, surely, surely have to understand the commingling of self-organization and selection. We will have to see that we are the natural expressions of a deeper order. Ultimately, we will discover in our creation myth that we are expected after all."

The young girl from Chapter 24 knows there is more to the picture. How ironic the Markets, with their greed and fear and envy and ruthless indifference, give us a portal into where and how to look.

Chapter 32

Conclusion. For Now...

There is a tide in the affairs of men.
Which, taken at the flood, leads on to fortune;
Omitted, all the voyage of their life
Is bound in shallows and in miseries.
On such a full sea are we now afloat,
And we must take the current when it serves,
Or lose our ventures. - William Shakespeare.

From the Bible's talk of feast and famine to the Tao's Yin and Yang, the message of boom and bust weaves through our myths. Those books foretold of our era centuries ago. We are the lucky ones. We hold the view of the capstone in our direct sight.

This universe exploded on the scene for a length of time beyond our comprehension. And now, 11 billion years since the networked web of galaxies formed, or the 4.5 billion years since our earth began spinning, or 3 billion years since life ignited its slow march, we sit in a seat that created the technology to ponder the passage of 5 major extinctions. These extinctions have paved the path for our wave of novelty and intelligence to form.

We now find ourselves at the crest of the sixth major epoch.

We have the knowledge, computer power, and sophistication to map out the capstone and its astonishing view.

The markets have collected the data of our progress like DNA collected the information of our ancestors. Because of the duration of the cycle, similar to a firmly established hurricane, we can calculate the path it will fulfill.

Humans produced a strange invention with the roller coaster. Of the myriad concerns we could occupy our time with, why compose such a ride. Maybe this ecstatic communal experience holds a cultural metaphor for what lies ahead.

We are fortunate to be alive when we can witness the most incredible economic ride ever built. Our ancestors lay behind us. The foundation sits below us. The view from the capstone's height compels us. The ups and downs await in front of us. Time to heed the message of the stock market and buckle up.

Select the wishing well best suited for our talents. Hold tight with gratitude for our part in the process. Accept the pain accompanying the journey. Let go of the penny, and enjoy the ride!

Epilogue

I came here tonight because when you realize you want to spend the rest of your life with somebody, you want the rest of your life to start as soon as possible. - When Harry Met Sally.

The first thought that comes to mind if anyone claims to predict the stock markets is: then why aren't you a billionaire and why would you tell anyone?

I'm no different from the fractals I've laid out here. Life is Yin and Yang and full of fat tails. The fat-tails in my life - both to the upside and the downside - contained a necessary part of building the stress to motivate the work. I've surfed the Edge of Chaos my entire life, and I have the successes and bruises to show for it.

I had a major extinction event, resulting in this book. I have every intention of compounding elite alpha with outlier Sharpe ratios as a testament and proof of the theory.

A short amount of time has passed since having my eureka moment with the use of the Feigenbaum constants. I've had the outline for over 20 years, but the guts came about since locking myself in a room after the world changed a year ago.

I have thought hard about the best action to take with this insight.

I'm not a member of the science community; I've been around the market my whole life. So a logical starting place would be the hedge fund industry. Compound my capital and retire into the sunset…

Working with a hedge fund holds out some special appeal. — Confirmation of the theory. Collaboration with bright minds. To extend and improve upon blind spots. And of course to produce tremendous amounts of capital. —

It appeals enough, that I have reached out to a few of the leading hedge funds. But something seemed off about leveraging my ideas with a small group of people.

And most aren't even open to this idea. They want to see proof in the profits. 5-year track records are a conservative norm. They like profits, not prophets.

I tried to start a fund myself back when I was young, naïve, less battle-scarred, and frankly too arrogant to succeed.

If I write the book first, the concept will make its way to multiple hedge funds. They will put their supercomputers to work and achieve insights not attainable if I went to work with only one. Keeping the information private and proprietary.

This may already exist in some proprietary hands? If so, what's the point of having valuable information for the profit of so few?

A logical second route leads to a similar outcome. Make massive capital gains, then use those resources to share how I did it.

This linear path leads to a larger platform. Currently, no one might care about my opinions. Even if they did, my platform or network may not get it executed.

I have opted to go with my intuition and write the book first. My role in the process belongs in getting the information out. This will lead to the leverage of ideas through collaboration and cooperation. This holds a better fit for me. Go nonlinear. Write the book first and see what happens. Who knows what will emerge.

Why wait five years and keep the information in only a few people's hands? We live in the age of information and I'm going to put it out there for anyone who wants to use it, criticize it, improve it, challenge it, or enjoy it.

We all take our places in the circle of life. I consider this mine.

I began with an epigraph from the Tao Te Ching, I'll end with the same passage from the same book. Different translation from a different translator. Same message, a different messenger. I will include both in their entirety so you can contrast the differences.

A perfect fractal of my book. I contributed little new material. I'm translating. The map of 2052, and the math confirming it, house my individual capstone. A humbling piece to add to the vast conversation. Hopefully, it holds value.

Along the way, I trust I relayed missives from a distinct voice touching you, the reader, in a fashion, it touched me.

Nothingness can be said to be Zero.
Zero births One.
One created Two.
Two births Three.
After that, only Zero can count what it Is.
But all breathe the Air of Nothingness.
All bathe in its Light.
Worldly success is a shade of illusion,
Painful in its Game.
Being an orphan is lonely,
Painful, too, in its Game.
Conquest is a step backward.
Begin counting again, but commence from Infinity.

Tao Te Ching– Verse 42
Translation by Jeremy M. Miller, 2013

The Tao gives birth to One.
One gives birth to Two.
Two gives birth to Three.
Three gives birth to all things.
All things have their backs to the female
and stand facing the male.
When male and female combine,
all things achieve harmony.
Ordinary men hate solitude.
But the Master makes use of it,
embracing his aloneness, realizing
he is one with the whole universe.

Tao Te Ching– Verse 42
Translation by Stephen Mitchell, 1995

For more information, visit our website @

ecstaticstocks.com

Feedback is an important part of any system. Please provide a review with Amazon to help with our process. Thank you.

Made in the USA
Columbia, SC
20 July 2021